Growing Together

Six Intergenerational Celebrations

Volume II
Spring & Summer

with contributions by
Kathy Finley
Sylvia DeVillers
Sara Fontana

Living the Good News
a division of The Morehouse Group

D1410425

An Acknowledgment

Growing Together incorporates the work of many unnamed contributors, as well as those listed here. We wish to acknowledge the many editors, writers, staff members and others whose vision, ideas and words enrich this resource for parish families.

© 2000 Living the Good News

Cover illustration: Teresa Flavin
Cover design: Jim Lemons
Illustrations: Sally Brewer Lawrence, Anne Kosel, Victoria Bergesen
Editor: Dina Strong Gluckstern

Scripture texts referred to in this work are taken from the *New Revised Standard Version Bible*, copyright © 1989 by the Division of Christian Education of the National Council of Churches of Christ in the USA, and are used by permission.

ISBN: 1-889108-46-4

Table of Contents

Introduction

Since our earliest days, **Living the Good News** has encouraged parishes to bring all ages together to worship, celebrate and learn. We believe that times spent together as a whole parish family can serve a three-fold purpose.

First, through such occasions we can become better acquainted with our parish family, young and old together. We can take steps toward making our parish the warm, nurturing community we long for in our fragmented world. Older adults who grew up in the pre-Vatican II Church sometimes feel a sense of displacement in parish life today. Celebrations and rituals help all generations find their own meanings in a common ground of experience.

Second, we can experience scripture and traditions in a fresh way that can give beauty and meaning to our daily lives. Third, and underlying all else, we can develop a more intimate relationship with God, who calls each of us by name.

In this volume of *Growing Together* we offer suggestions for organizing six sessions focusing on:
- Mardi Gras Carnival
- Lent
- Easter
- Pentecost
- Summer Celebration of God's Creation
- Assumption

The first volume of *Growing Together* is also available and contains six more celebrations: Building a Church Family, All Saints, Thanksgiving, Advent, Christmas and Epiphany. In this volume, we repeat our introductory material to give leaders an overview of how to organize successful gatherings of all ages.

In each chapter you will find far more than enough activities for a one-hour session. This abundance allows you to choose only those activities that meet your parish's particular needs and fit its schedule.

Our hope is that, in a small way, this book will help the Body of Christ grow in understanding and "build itself up through love" (Ephesians 4:16).

Why Gather All Ages Together?

Many of our experiences in life happen when several generations are together. Vacations, trips, holidays and family events are shared by old and young alike. We tend to separate people by ages mainly for education and employment.

Many parish programs make this same separation of generations, but more and more catechists and religious educators are recommending programs in which adults and children learn together.

Growing Together is designed to meet the need for generations to learn together. This approach requires that we venture beyond traditional learning methods into the world of experiential learning.

What Is Experiential Learning?

In *Growing Together* you will find ideas for experiences that involve the whole person rather than the intellect alone. These experiences include, but are by no means limited to, art, movement activities, writing simple poems, making quick paper banners and various outreach projects.

Experiential learning is the way we learn in real life. It is the way that young children acquire an amazing "data base" of skills and information in the first few years of life. (From ages 2 to 4, our vocabularies alone grow from about 50 words to 10,000 or more.) Experiential learning is how we learned to speak and how any of us have learned most of what we know.

Experiential learning takes us beyond a nodding acquaintance with new ideas and allows us to make them our own. Though it does not rely heavily on such methods as reciting, taking notes on a lecture or writing objective answers in blanks, neither is it incapable of communicating objective, factual information. The activities in *Growing Together* are balanced to teach specific content *and* evoke intuitive, feeling responses.

You have probably heard the maxim: I hear and I forget; I see and I remember; I do and I understand. The more of our-selves (body, mind and spirit) we can use to explore an idea, the more the idea becomes our own.

Similarly, Jesus understood that the more of ourselves we bring into relationship with God, the more intimate and enduring this relationship becomes. He taught that we are not far from the kingdom of heaven if we love God with all our hearts, all our souls, all our minds and all our strength.

Thus, experiential learning in a Christian setting beckons us to sing, dance and clap. It beckons us to construct a scale model or act out a skit. It beckons us to play. We use experiential methods because they:

- rely on other modalities of learning rather than the intellect alone.
- involve the whole person: senses, emotions, mind and spirit.
- make learning a thing to enjoy and internalize.
- provide opportunities for students to discover and use their talents, to learn to work together harmoniously and to develop skills of leadership and creativity.
- welcome the Holy Spirit to lead us to unexpected insights.

Experiential methods require careful planning and sometimes more effort than preparing a lecture. But inviting parish members to participate fully in their own education can produce a rich harvest of responsible attitudes, sound conceptual learning and joy for both catechists and students.

Growing Together

When Can You Use These Sessions?

In a typical parish, consider using these sessions as:

- parish intergenerational programs
- seasonal parish family gatherings
- primary religious education material for a small parish
- supplementary material for large parish religious education programs
- supplementary material for religion classes in Catholic schools
- home-study religious education programs
- RCIA social gatherings for adults and children
- catechetical sessions for children preparing for Christian Initiation
- small Christian communities or base communities
- incorporation into family sacramental programs

Finding time and resources to add another component to already full schedules, both in families and in parish organizations, can be a challenge. Family-centered gatherings and Christian Initiation groups of all kinds have fewer constraints in following tightly-scheduled curriculums.

Look to different groups in the parish who could successfully host an intergenerational gathering. One promising lead would be to invite parish youth organizations to be in charge of leading one or more sessions. Consider also the possibility of asking a different parish organization to host a different session. Use our session planning pages as an organizing tool for host teams.

How Do You Plan a Session?

In each chapter of *Growing Together* you will find several **Key Ideas** and a cluster of activities that teach each **Key Idea**. When planning a one-hour session, *you will need to choose only a few of these activities*. Ask yourself:

- Which key ideas in this chapter are most important for our parish to explore?
- Which of the suggested activities will best help us to explore these key ideas?
- Which activities best fit our schedule?
- Which activities best fit the diverse ages and learning styles of our congregation?

What Materials Will You Need?

We know that not every parish can allocate generous funds for Christian education. We welcome the educational potential of such equipment as video cameras and tape recorders, but we do not assume all parishes can afford them. The materials in this book are simple and inexpensive.

Each activity includes a list of materials needed. Materials common to many *Growing Together* sessions include:

> Bibles
> chalkboard and chalk or newsprint
> and marker
> felt pens
> crayons, regular and oversized for
> young children

drawing paper
glue
scissors

How Can Prayer Play a Lively Part?

Most of us have had rich experiences with corporate prayer in the context of our parish worship. Many of us also have private prayer lives that nourish us, deepening our relationship to God and to our innermost selves.

For some of us this private prayer time is structured and consistent in time and place. For others it may be spontaneous and less formal. Fewer of us have prayed together comfortably and spontaneously with other members of our parish in an informal setting. A true blessing of parish gatherings with all ages together is the growing ability to pray together, rejoicing in the presence of God and God's people gathered.

You can begin your parish family sessions with prayer and close with prayer. As a sense of community begins to develop through working together, certain moments will call forth the desire to pray together right then with no worry as to having just the proper words.

Here are various suggestions for closing prayers; you will find more at the end of each chapter:

- Plan your session with time for unhurried prayer. Do not worry if the younger children prefer to wander around at this time. They will still hear and be part of the prayer.

- Pass out songbooks and sing together as a closing prayer.
- Supply small pieces of paper, pencils and a basket. As people arrive, invite them to write prayer requests on the slips of paper and place them in the basket. At the end of the session the leader includes the prayer requests in the closing prayer.
- Bring into the center of your prayer circle the fruits of your session: the art work created, props used in a skit, etc. Ask the group to quietly reflect on insights they have gained from the session. As leader, offer your own thanksgivings and allow time for others to do likewise.
- Once you sense that people want to offer their thoughts aloud, here is a simple, safe way to invite extemporaneous prayers. Form a circle with everyone holding hands. Explain that you are going to offer a brief prayer and that when you are finished, you will squeeze the hand of the person to your right.

That person either offers a prayer aloud or chooses to remain silent, then squeezes the hand of the next person as a signal for the next person to continue.

- Invite a small group of volunteers to spend a few minutes with you preparing the closing prayer. This prayer can take the form of music, dance, art or even mime. Or one of the activities a small group completed during your session could be presented to your whole parish family as a prayer.

Growing Together

How Can You Group the Participants?

One satisfying way to group participants in parish family sessions is by offering a choice of activities, each in its own room or corner. Prepare half-a-dozen activities for your session, and briefly present the choices to the participants. Ask participants to choose more than one activity, so that you can rotate the groups during the hour.

One parish using this method allowed participants to choose freely between several activities: watching a film made by intermediate participants, decorating a processional cross, discussing the day's liturgical rites, conducting a movement session (especially appropriate for the youngest children) and learning a hymn appropriate for the day.

Another method is to break into temporary and arbitrary groups as needed for particular activities. This can be done by counting off, by color of name tags, month of birthday or in some other way.

Some parishes have felt more secure with long-term groups. Some make pairs of an adult and a child and then form groups by combining pairs. Other parishes have established "families" or "tribes" of mixed ages who work together on group assignments.

How Can You Integrate Children Into Parish Family Sessions?

Successful parish family programs help children to be participants, not onlookers. Planning must therefore take into account children's learning needs, their limited reading skills, spoken vocabularies, dexterity and attention spans. The activities and methods of presentation should be chosen with these things in mind.

Since you want the children to be integrated into the group, you will **not** want to provide child-size tables and chairs. You **will** want to encourage everyone to help the children see, hear and take part.

For example, if each person is to write something on a 3" x 5" card, some adult should write what a youngster wants to say. If you plan to make drawings, it helps to provide crayons of both regular and kindergarten size.

When an activity calls for oral answers or group discussion, the leader will want to be careful to protect the children's right to participate. The leader should caution adults not to put words in the children's mouths, answer for them or ignore them.

If your session includes preschoolers, you may want to set up a corner with paper and crayons, play dough and blocks. Then as the session unfolds, the children can choose whether to work in their own corner or to participate with the larger group. You will most likely find that the adults enjoy and learn much from the fresh outlook and abounding faith of the children.

What Activities Work Best for All Ages Together?

Brainstorming

Often an activity will say "Brainstorm a list of ways to..." or "Brainstorm the kinds of feelings you have when..."

Brainstorming means having everyone throw out ideas in rapid succession. Be sure everyone knows that the rules of the game are:

- Do not judge or evaluate ideas.
- Do not wait to be called on; just speak up.
- Add on to what others say.

The leader or someone else should list all ideas on chalkboard or newsprint. The values of brainstorming are:

- It gets everyone to offer ideas.
- Some "way-out" ideas often can lead to a fresh way to look at something.
- It is a good way to get people to open up and start talking.
- If you are looking for a way to do something, you may find it by combining several ideas from the list.

If you need to teach a group how to brainstorm, you might explain the process and then let members try it on a topic such as "How many ways can we use a newspaper?"

Drama, Dance, Movement

Creative movement, dance, drama, mime and story telling are excellent ways to present scripture in parish family sessions. Another approach is "readers' theater," the dramatic reading of a story from scripture by a narrator and others who read the parts of the various characters. (You might want to give the audience a part as well, maybe sound effects or cheering for the hero!)

Some of the activities in *Growing Together* suggest dramatizations of incidents from scripture, with the players making up their own dialogue. These informal skits provide an enjoyable way for participants to see the details, as well as the emotional content, of an incident. At other times, groups are asked to plan and present a brief skit on some real life situation related to a key idea.

In a parish family session, drama in all its forms should be done in a spontaneous fashion—no memorizing of lines or elaborate props and costumes. Encourage participants to project themselves into the scene and to use their own words to express feelings and ideas. If a group chooses to put a biblical event in a modern setting, welcome current idioms of speech and humor.

Enjoying a learning experience makes it a memorable encounter. Humor is one key; sometimes laughing at human folly produces that "Aha!" experience, when suddenly we come to a new realization about ourselves.

Dramatized stories, concepts taught through movement, parables enacted in modern settings—all communicate the word in lively, engaging fashion. Incorporating the dramatic arts in Christian education helps us discover that we are indeed co-creators with God.

These methods allow all ages to work, talk, play and create together. They provide an arena in which individuals may express who they really are. Such a shared experience engages us directly with scripture, evoking insights that can inspire significant change and growth.

Music

"Make a joyful noise to the Lord, all the lands! Serve the Lord with gladness! Come into his presence with singing!" (Psalm 100:1)

Quiet, peaceful music draws us into a prayerful attitude, while bright, rousing music stirs us to express joy and praise. Music belongs to all phases of Christian celebration, but especially in parish family sessions. It is a medium that appeals to old and young alike. It can set the mood for a session, or change the mood to prepare for a change of activity.

Sometimes you may want to invite youngsters to teach a song they have learned in their class. You can invite music ministers to teach a song or to lead a hymn-sing. You can ask volunteers to prepare a mime, a movement activity or a liturgical dance to accompany a song sung by the whole parish family.

To encourage singing, use songs familiar to the participants. If children are participating, you can coordinate the music with that used in their parish religious education classes.

Art

Art is an important channel through which all ages may express their understandings, beliefs and feelings. In fact, through participation in art, a person's understandings may deepen and come into focus. Many people can express ideas more readily in a visual way than by verbal means. Not least of all, art in individual or cooperative form can be satisfying and fun.

The attitudes with which art activities are handled will in great measure affect the participants' responses. Acceptance of everyone's art, based on respect for individual and developmental differences, is essential.

Encourage creativity. (Coloring within the lines is not important!) Take care not to impose your own way of seeing the world on others; avoid competition and comparison. Ask everyone to try the art activities, explaining that in this setting, producing a great work of art is not important.

Creating something of meaning to one's self is the object. (A work of art that opens a new door to its maker may also speak to others in your parish family.) Creating art may also be an act of worship.

Parish family members will be more likely to experiment with art if the leader is working right along with the group. Value each person's contribution, making a real effort to listen to what a person is saying through art.

Other Ways to Use
Growing Together

We suggest sharing *Growing Together* with catechists, who may want to use some of its activities in age-graded religious education settings. Catechists will also appreciate the chapter introductions, which provide concise summaries of seasons and feasts, and the bibliography of valuable resources for religious educators.

Sara Fontana of St. Paul's in Houston suggests, "The Parent Advisory Committee at St. Paul's and myself developed a wonderful process that we call CCE Family Days. CCE in the Galveston-Houston Diocese stands for Continuing Christian Education (equivalent to CCD in other places). The Family Day starts with everyone together for a short, upbeat opening and sing-along. After the opening, families choose centers which last anywhere from 15 to 25 minutes. In the time span we allow families can usually choose up to four centers. The family travels together, and each of the centers is geared to individuals from three years of age to grandparents.

"This year we will be having two CCE Family Days. One will be focused on Advent and one will be focused on Lent. I will be using the *Growing Together* activities as ideas for the centers.

The wonderful thing about doing centers is that a presenter does the same thing four or five times. The presentation is short and extremely "do-able" for people's busy lives. Especially when we have resources such as *Growing Together!*"

Mardi Gras Carnival

Introduction and Information

Although popular etymology translates the word *carnival* as "Carnem, vale," (literally, farewell, meat) the word more likely comes from the Latin phrase *carnem levare:* the removal of meat. Medieval Christians developed carnivals to celebrate with exuberance one last time before the rigorous Lenten fast.

Although Lenten regulations varied with time and place, no meat, butter, eggs, milk, or cheese were generally allowed during the 40 days. Lenten meals might be restricted to one each day and that one taken after sundown.

In addition to fasting, Christians were permitted no weddings, dances, or festivals during Lent; the season was reserved for prayer and penance. So medieval Christians began to observe days of celebration, to hold rowdy parades, masquerades, and dances, and to fling themselves into festivity one last time before Lent.

Festivity and Feasting

Such pre-Lenten festivities are still widely observed today, preserved in the gondola parades of Venice, the Mardi Gras floats of New Orleans, and the street parties of Rio de Janeiro.

Recipes for all manner of rich foods that medieval Christians consumed during Carnival have been preserved in various pre-Lenten traditions. Such feasting developed in part to prepare body and spirit for the long fast and in part to use up the foods that could not be stored during Lent.

Doughnuts filled with raisins and apples were one of the first European carnival foods to become popular in America. These delicious cakes, brought by Dutch and German settlers, are still prepared by Pennsylvania Dutch families today.

More widely known are the pancakes eaten in several countries: English Shrove Tuesday pancakes, French crepes, and Russian blini.

Rich foods give Carnival days many colorful names—Butter Week, Fat Days, and Fat Tuesday. Another name, Shrove Tuesday, is derived from a different custom: that of confessing sins (being *shriven*) in order to begin the spiritual battle of Lent renewed by an awareness of God's power and mercy.

Such a time of confession carries with it a spirit of sorrow and contrition over sin. For this reason, the word *alleluia* is omitted from Lenten liturgies and restored again during the celebrations of Easter. A Mardi Gras celebration provides an excellent opportunity to bid farewell to this joyous word.

Growing Together

Both confession and festival are still excellent ways to prepare for Lent. Perhaps we, too, can find in confession a renewal of joy in God's forgiveness. Perhaps we, too, can find in festival a renewal of foolishness and fun with our Christian brothers and sisters.

Perhaps we, too, can prepare ourselves to take Lent more seriously by giving ourselves permission to feast and play beforehand. Perhaps we, too, can plunge gaily into Carnival, and emerge prepared for a holy Lent.

Alleluia

Help! How do I plan this session?

How will I publicize this session?

_____

_____

How many people do I think might participate? _____

What are the ages of the participants?

_____

Where will we hold the session?

_____

Which recommended activities would work best with this particular group of participants? (Remember, we provide more activities than most groups can use in a single session. Pick a few that will work for your group.)

_____

_____

_____

_____

_____

_____

_____

_____

Volunteers

to do	names	phone numbers
planning:		
preparation and set-up:		
activity leaders:		
clean-up:		

Session Plan

Gathering Prayer

Use the "Blessing for a Family or Household" from Catholic Household Blessings and Prayers, p. 206-210 or sing together a favorite hymn that includes the praise "alleluia."

Key Idea

Carnival foods are usually rich, providing final treats before Lent and using up foods not eaten during Lent. Pancakes are traditional pre-Lenten food in many countries.

Small Group Activity: Shrove Tuesday Pancakes

Materials

2-1/2 cups flour
1-1/4 teaspoons baking soda
1 teaspoon salt
1 egg
3 cups buttermilk
4-6 tablespoons butter
honey
syrup

Other materials:
sifter
2 mixing bowls
mixing spoon
small cup
10"-12" cast iron skillet or griddle
spatula
plates
forks

This Anglo-American recipe makes about 18-24 pancakes.

Directions: Sift the flour, baking soda, and salt into a mixing bowl. In the other bowl, beat together the egg and buttermilk. Pour the egg and buttermilk mixture into the flour and stir until no dry flour is visible.

Heat the skillet or griddle over medium high heat, until a drop of water flicked on the griddle's surface sizzles. Remove the pan from the heat and put in 2 tablespoons of butter. When the butter is melted, add it to the pancake batter and stir the batter to mix in the butter.

Dip a small cup in the batter and pour four pancakes into the skillet. Bubbles will form on the surface of each pancake. Cook until the surfaces look dry. Use a spatula to turn the pancakes. Cook about one minute more. Remove the pancakes, spread 1 teaspoon of butter in the skillet, and spoon in four more pancakes. Serve the cooked pancakes with honey or syrup.

Small Group Activity: Mardi Gras Crepes

Materials

3 eggs
1-1/2 cups milk
1 cup flour
1/2 teaspoon salt
4-5 tablespoons butter
powdered sugar
jam
jelly

Other materials:

blender
6"-7" crepe pan
1/2-cup measure
spatula
spoons
plates
forks

This French recipe makes 20-24 crepes, the traditional French pancake for Mardi Gras.

Directions: Blend the eggs and milk in the blender. Add the flour and salt and blend again.

Heat the crepe pan over medium high heat until a drop of water flicked on the pan's surface sizzles. Remove the pan from the heat and put in two tablespoons of butter. When the butter is melted, add it to the crepe batter and blend again.

Spoon 3 tablespoons of batter into the crepe pan. (Use a 1/4-cup measure for this step. Estimate the amount of batter needed to fill three-quarters of the measure.) Swirl the pan quickly, spreading the batter over the bottom.

Cook over medium high heat until the surface looks dry and the edges look crisp. Use a spatula to turn the crepe and cook one minute more.

Remove the crepe, melt 1 teaspoon of butter in the pan, and add the batter for the next crepe. To serve one crepe, put a spoon of jelly or jam in a thin line down the center of the crepe. Roll the crepe into a cylinder and sprinkle it with powdered sugar.

Note: Older children and adults may enjoy the French Mardi Gras custom of turning the crepe by flipping it into the air and catching it with the pan. According to tradition, successful turning brings good luck for the coming year.

Small Group Activity: Butter Week Blini

Materials

1 cup milk
1 tablespoon sugar
1 cup lukewarm water
1 tablespoon *or* 1 packet *or* 1 cake yeast
1-1/2 cups whole wheat flour
1 teaspoon salt
2 eggs
4 tablespoons soft butter
1 cup buckwheat flour
cream of tartar
salt
melted butter

Growing Together

sour cream
hard-cooked eggs, chopped

Other materials:
  saucepan
  cup
  3 mixing bowls
  mixing spoon
  plate
  either a balloon whisk or an electric
    mixer
  rubber spatula
  10"-12" skillet or griddle
  spatula
  plates
  forks

Note: This recipe makes several dozen blini, the traditional Butter Week pancakes of Russia. The entire recipe takes about six hours to make, but most of that time is for letting the batter rise. If necessary, start the recipe in the morning or afternoon **before the session** and refrigerate the batter after either of the two rising periods. At the session let the batter return to room temperature before proceeding with the next step in the recipe.

Directions: Scald the milk in a saucepan and then let it cool until it is lukewarm. In a cup, dissolve the sugar in 1/2 cup lukewarm water. Sprinkle the yeast onto the water and let rest five minutes. Mix the yeast into the scalded milk, and add the remaining 3/4 cup of water. Beat in the whole wheat flour and the teaspoon of salt. Beat until smooth. Cover with a plate and let rise at room temperature until light, about two hours.

Stir down the batter. Separate the eggs. Cream the soft butter; then blend in the egg yolks. Beat the butter mixture into the batter, together with 1 cup of buckwheat flour. Let rise again for two hours.

Stir down the batter. Use a balloon whisk or an electric mixer to beat the two egg whites, adding a pinch of cream of tartar and a pinch of salt. Beat until the egg whites are stiff. Use a rubber spatula to fold the egg whites into the batter.

Heat the skillet or griddle until a drop of water flicked on the skillet's surface sizzles. Spread a teaspoon of butter in the pan. Spoon five to eight tiny pancakes in the pan.

Cook until their surfaces look dry; then use a spatula to turn the blini. Cook them one minute more. Repeat until the batter is gone. Serve the cooked blini with melted butter, sour cream, and chopped hard-cooked egg.

Small Group Activity: "Pancake" Relay

Materials

  Frisbees or plastic coffee can lids, 1 per
    team
  paper or plastic dinner plates, 1 per
    team

Note: Many countries have pancake races and games, but hot pancakes and skillets are unsafe for young children. This game uses plastic "pancakes" as substitutes.

Divide the participants into relay teams, with six to eight participants on each team. Give the starting participant from each team a plastic "pancake" and a paper or plastic dinner plate.

Have each starting participant, with a "pancake" on the plate, run to a finish line and then back to the team. Have the participants use their plates to flip the "pancakes" as they run. Set a minimum number of flips—perhaps six on the way to the turning point and six on the return trip.

As each participant returns to the team, he or she should hand the "pancake" and plate to the next participant. The first team to have all of its members complete the trip wins the relay.

Leader's Resources: Outreach

- Participants could be asked to bring an item of "rich and delicious" carnival-type food, such as donuts, fancy cookies, pastries, etc., for distribution to the hungry or poor. For the poor, many of their daily meals are meager and austere. A special treat would make a welcome change.
- Mardi Gras is rich in food traditions. Consider staging the Mardi Gras celebration at a local homeless shelter or food kitchen. A "Mardi Gras Pancake Supper" could be prepared for the evening meal.

Key Idea

Costumes and masquerades are common to many pre-Lenten carnival celebrations.

Small Group Activity: Carnival Face-Painting Center

Materials

cold cream
either stage make-up or assorted
    cosmetics in bright colors
tissues
mirrors
Optional:
white zinc oxide salve

Note: Greasepaint crayons are inexpensive and effective make-up tools. Look for them at a toy or costume store.

Set up a center where participants can paint their faces with make-up. Encourage older participants to offer help to younger participants.

Directions to participants applying make-up to themselves or others: Begin with a thin layer of cold cream to protect the skin and to simplify make-up removal. If desired, use zinc oxide salve to make a white base for a clown face.

Growing Together

Clown make-up uses bright colors and bold shapes to emphasize an actual facial expression or emotion. A happy face might be indicated by broad red lines drawn *around* the lips, bright triangles of color on the cheeks, and black, arching lines *over* the eyebrows.

You may prefer to make an animal face, complete with whiskers. Another option is to use abstract designs and patterns to create as beautiful or frightening or mysterious a face as you want.

▶ Small Group Activity: Costume Charades

Materials

box of assorted items for improvising costumes: cloth, towels, safety pins, cardboard tubes, sticks, hats, rope, string, toy tools, etc.

Note: Preschool and kindergarten children probably will not be able to guess words with much success, but younger children can still enjoy the game if they are given parts to act out and are allowed to guess freely.

Divide the participants into several teams. One team is designated the *acting* team and the other teams are designated *guessing* teams.

Directions to the teams: The acting team leaves the room and picks a word to act out. The word should have three or four syllables, such as *marketplace*.

The acting team should devise skits to portray each syllable, plus a final skit to portray the whole word. *Marketplace* would need four skits: one for *mark*, one for *cat*, one for *place*, and one for *marketplace*. The acting team may use the box of items to improvise simple costumes.

One member of the acting team must announce each skit as it is performed, by saying, for example, "second syllable," or "whole word."

Each guessing team should confer quietly between skits, trying to guess the acted syllable or word. When all the skits have been completed, each guessing team should decide on *one* guess. The guessing team that answers correctly, or comes closest to answering correctly, becomes the next acting team.

▶ Small Group Activity: Costume Stories

Materials

shopping bags
items for improvising costumes: cloth, towels, cardboard tubes, sticks, hats, rope, string, toy tools, etc.
3" x 5" index cards
pens or pencils
basket

Before the session fill six shopping bags with items for improvising costumes. Make sure each bag has a diverse collection of items.

At the session distribute the index cards. Ask each participant to write the name of an animal or the title of a human profession or job on the card. Collect the cards in a basket.

Divide the participants into six teams. Pass around the basket and ask each participant to take one card. Each participant will play the part written on the index card in a short skit.

Give each team a shopping bag with costume items. Allow 10 minutes for each team to devise a skit, incorporating the roles of that team's participants. Allow another five minutes for each team to improvise costumes for its members from the items in the team's shopping bag. Have the teams take turns presenting the skits.

Small Group Activity: Scavenger Hunt

Materials

> copies of the Costume Scavenger Hunt List, found at the end of this activity
> pens or pencils

Note: This scavenger hunt requires that participants come to the Carnival in costume.

Divide the participants into teams of four to six members each. Give each team a copy of the Costume Scavenger Hunt List and a pen or pencil.

Directions to the teams: Take your list and find participants whose costumes match the items listed. Write the participants'

names next to the appropriate items. For example, if a participant named Dana Smith wore a red mask, you could write "Dana Smith" next to *a costume with something red*.

Find one participant for each item listed. No participant's name can be used twice. The team that finds the most items listed wins the Hunt.

Costume Scavenger Hunt List

1. A costume with something red
   _____

2. A costume that uses elastic
   _____

3. A costume made from paper
   _____

4. A costume with sequins
   _____

5. A costume with purple or green
   _____

6. A costume with fur
   _____

7. A costume that covers the neck
   _____

8. A costume that bares the arms
   _____

9. A costume of an animal
   _____

10. A costume with stripes
    _____

11. A costume with high heels
    _____

12. A costume that is black

    _____

13. A costume with polka dots

    _____

14. A costume that is fuzzy

    _____

15. A costume that is hard

    _____

16. A costume with buttons

    _____

17. A costume that is shiny

    _____

18. A costume with orange or pink

    _____

19. A costume with a crown

    _____

20. A costume with an umbrella

    _____

Key Idea

Carnival celebrations are usually noisy—even rowdy—in contrast to the quiet, reflective season of Lent that follows.

Small Group Activity: Making Noisemakers

Set up a center where participants can make a variety of simple noisemakers.

Humming Combs

Materials

    plastic combs
    waxed paper

Directions to the participants: Fold a piece of waxed paper in half. Place the comb inside the paper so that the tines touch the fold. Hold the comb to your lips and hum.

Cardboard Kazoo

Materials

    cardboard tubes
    waxed paper
    scissors
    rubber bands
    Optional:
    construction paper or tissue paper
       in various colors
    scissors
    crayons or felt markers
    crepe paper streamers
    glue
    sequins or glitter

Directions to the participants: Cut a 4" square of waxed paper and fit it over the end of a cardboard tube. Secure the waxed paper with a rubber band. Hum into the open end of the tube.

If participants wish, they may decorate their kazoos with construction or tissue paper, crayons or felt markers, crepe paper streamers, glue, and sequins or glitter. Younger participants may be given the responsibility for decorating the instruments as the adults make them.

Box Rattles

Materials

empty cardboard oatmeal boxes with
covers

small noise-making materials, such as
rice, beans, pebbles, etc.

masking tape

Optional:

construction paper or tissue paper in
various colors

scissors

crayons or felt markers

crepe paper streamers

glue

sequins or glitter

Directions to the participants: Fill an
empty oatmeal box with a handful of rice,
beans, pebbles, etc. Secure the cover with
a strip of masking tape.

If participants wish, they may decorate
their rattles with construction or tissue
paper, crayons or felt markers, crepe paper streamers, glue, and sequins or glitter.
Younger participants may be given the responsibility for decorating the instruments
as the adults make them.

Bell Circles

Materials

scissors or pocket knife

plastic lids (such as those used on
coffee cans)

pipe cleaners, 4 per lid

inexpensive bells for sewing, 4 per lid

Directions to the participants: Use the
scissors or pocketknife to punch four

holes in a plastic lid. Use the pipe cleaners
to attach one bell to each hole.

Cymbals

Materials

pairs of pot lids

Directions to the participants: Bang two
pot lids together like cymbals.

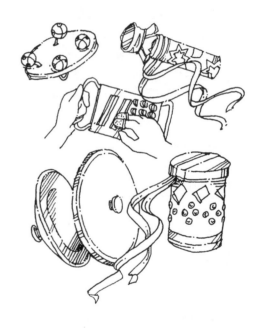

Rasp

Materials

metal thimbles

metal cheese graters

Directions to the participants: Put one or
more thimbles on the fingers of one hand.
Use the thimbles to rasp a metal cheese
grater held in the other hand.

Growing Together

Small Group Activity: Noisy Handkerchief

Materials

assorted noisemakers (see above)
handkerchief

Ask each participant to select one noise-maker. Ask the participants to sit in a circle. Select one participant to be the first leader.

Ask the leader to stand in the center of the circle, holding the handkerchief up high. Tell the participants to *begin* making noise when the leader drops the handkerchief and to *stop* making noise when the handkerchief touches the floor.

Players who begin too soon, stop too soon, or stop too late are *out*. The last player *in* becomes the next leader.

Small Group Activity: Noisy Chairs

Materials

assorted noisemakers (see above)
chairs

Invite participants to play this variation of *Musical Chairs*. Line up the chairs in two rows, back-to-back, providing three fewer chairs than the number of participants.

Take a noisemaker and begin making noise. Have the participants walk in a single line around the rows of chairs. When you stop the noise, each participant must try to sit down in a chair.

The participants who could not find chairs join you in making noise for the next round. (Agree on a signal, such as mouthing the word *now*, for stopping the noise.) Remove two more chairs and begin the noise.

Continue until only one participant is left. This participant can be the leader of the noise-making for the next round.

Large Group Activity: Treats Parade

Materials

treats, bikes and wagons (see **note** below)
decorations: tape, streamers, ribbons, balloons, etc.
wrapped candy
inexpensive party favors

Note: This activity, adapted from a neighborhood tradition started by Sara Fontana of St. Paul's Catholic Church in Houston, Texas, requires preparation **before the session**. Ask families to bring all the treats or "junk food" in their house to the carnival. Children also bring their bikes and wagons.

In the session, invite children to first decorate their bikes and wagons. Then invite children to ride their bikes and pull their wagons in a designated circular pattern. Invite older children, teenagers and adults to stand outside this circle area and throw candy and prizes. The children continue to ride until all the treats have been thrown.

Call out a signal for the children to run around and pick up candy and prizes.

Key Idea

A Carnival celebration provides an appropriate time to bid farewell to *alleluia*, a word generally omitted from Lenten liturgies.

Large Group Activity: Alleluia Sing

Materials

copies of hymnals
musical instrument(s)

Before the session arrange with one or more musicians to lead the participants in a hymn sing.

At the session invite participants to sing favorite hymns with *alleluia* one last time before Lent. Hymns could include traditional folk songs, such as "Michael, Row the Boat Ashore" or contemporary hymns, such as "Alleluia #1". The hymn sing could appropriately be concluded by singing, "Alleluia, Song of Gladness". This is the traditional pre-Lenten hymn of farewell to *alleluia*.

Leader's Resources: Multicultural Issues

- Teach and sing a variety of "Alleluia" music from various cultural traditions: African American, Vietnamese and Hispanic. *Suggestions:*
  — "El Senor Ha Resucitado" by Orlando Alturas
  — "Aleluya" by Carlos Rosas
  — "Alleluia" by Donna Pena
  — "Alleluia! Give the Glory!" by Ken Canedo
  — "The Celtic Alleluia" by Fintan O'Carroll and Christopher Walker
- Invite participants to share any Carnival foods from their family traditions. Be sure to include delicious *pan dulce*, a sweet cake-like bread from Mexico, as part of the session's refreshments.

Small Group Activity: Alleluia Poster

Materials

28" x 40" poster board
scissors
assorted papers: tissue, construction, colored foil, etc.
glue
felt pens
assorted decorations: dried flowers, sequins, glitter, ribbons, yarn, pompons, feathers, etc.

Invite participants to make and decorate an *alleluia* poster. Ask eight participants to write (or cut out letters for) the word *alleluia*, each participant writing one letter. The word should be centered on the poster.

Letters can be cut from paper and glued to the poster board, outlined in felt pen and filled with a glued collage material such as sequins, or drawn with felt pens alone.

Ask the other participants to create a decorative border, 4 to 6 inches wide, around the edge of the poster board. This border can combine drawings with such decorations as flowers, glitter, ribbons, etc.

Put the finished poster on display until the end of carnival. Then bid farewell to the *alleluia* with the service below.

Large Group Activity: Farewell to Alleluia Service

Materials

Alleluia Poster (see above)
copies of the *Farewell to Alleluia Service*, (below)
hymnals

Optional:
1 cloth, large enough to veil the Alleluia Poster

Note: This service includes a procession. Ask one participant to carry the Alleluia Poster in the procession. Ask other participants to carry noisemakers. Invite two participants to serve as readers.

Before the session find out where the Alleluia Poster can be stored until Easter. Appropriate possibilities include closets, sacristies, or side-chapels. If the poster will be visible during Lent, procure a cloth to veil the poster at the designated moment in the service.

To begin the service, gather around the Alleluia Poster.

Leader:
O God, make speed to save us, alleluia, alleluia.

Participants:
O Lord, make haste to help us, alleluia, alleluia.

Hymn:
(Select a hymn from those recommended for the Alleluia Hymn Sing, above.)

Reader #1:
After this I heard what seemed to be the loud voice of a great multitude in heaven, saying, "Hallelujah! Salvation and glory and power belong to our God."

And the twenty-four elders and the four living creatures fell down and worshiped

God who is seated on the throne, saying, "Amen. Hallelujah!" And from the throne there came a voice saying, "Praise our God, all you his servants, and all who fear him, small and great."

Then I heard what seemed to be the voice of a great multitude, like the sound of many waters and like the sound of mighty thunderpeals, crying out, "Hallelujah! For the Lord our God the Almighty reigns." (Revelation 19:1, 4-6)

(Form a procession to carry the Alleluia Poster to its resting place for Lent. Encourage participants to use their noisemakers and to shout *alleluia* while walking in procession. When you have reached the resting place, resume the readings.)

Leader:

Let us pray, reading aloud Psalm 137: 1-6.

Participants:

By the rivers of Babylon—
there we sat down and there we wept,
when we remembered Zion.

On the willows there
we hung up our harps.
For there our captors
asked us for songs,
and our tormentors called for mirth,
    saying,
"Sing us one of the songs of Zion!"

How could we sing the Lord's song
in a foreign land?
If I forget you, O Jerusalem,
let my right hand wither!

Let my tongue cling to the roof of my
    mouth
if I do not remember you,
if I do not set Jerusalem
above my highest joy. (Psalm 137:1-6)

(Silently put away or veil the Alleluia Poster.)

Leader:

Let us pray.

The Our Father

Leader:

God, you teach us to sing in praise. You teach us to pray in silence. Help us who prepare for the season to Lent to come with joy to the celebration of Easter, through Jesus Christ our Lord. *Amen*.

(It is appropriate for the participants to depart from the Carnival celebration in silence at the conclusion of this service.)

Closing Prayer

- If you use the Farewell to Alleluia Service, you can close with its final prayer.
- Ask everyone to sit comfortably on chairs or the floor. Invite participants to pray together the Our Father.
- Pray for those who will participate in RCIA in your parish this Lent.

Lent

Introduction and Information

Lent comes from an Old English word meaning lengthen. It is the season of late winter and early spring, the season when the days lengthen. Just as spring brings both the last bleak days of winter and the first green promise of summer, Lent brings a season of austerity and hope to Christians. The 40 days of Lent, beginning on Ash Wednesday and ending on Holy Saturday, call us to self-denial and discipline: a solemn preparation for the celebration of Easter.

The Feast of Easter is a baptismal feast, the preferred date for the administration of the sacrament of baptism, as was customary in the early Church. Converts to Christianity in the early Church completed their catechumenate with a time of preparation preceding their Easter baptism. This preparation was marked by fasting, prayer, and instruction.

Those who had been separated from the Church because of serious sin were expected to undertake a similar regime as a sign of penance before being welcomed back into the household of God. Roman ritual in the sixth century set the first day of Lent on a Wednesday (to provide 40 weekdays of Lent) and held a public dismissal of penitents from the Church on that day.

Forty Days of Preparation

Many of the faithful began joining the converts and penitents in this time of special discipline, as a sign of support and as a means of spiritual renewal. All three groups could look to the example of Jesus and, in particular, to his 40 days in the wilderness when he fasted and prayed as a preparation for his active ministry.

There are many other 40-day or 40-year periods of significance in Jewish history that also serve as foundational aspects of our Lenten period of preparation. Noah and his family witnessed, and were saved through, God's cleansing flood (Genesis 7:12). Moses fasted for 40 days and nights before he received the Ten Commandments (Deuteronomy 9:9). The Israelites wandered in the wilderness for 40 years before they entered God's promised land (Deuteronomy 8:2). Elijah traveled for 40 days until he reached the mountain of God (1 Kings 19:8).

Rite of Christian Initiation of Adults

In our own day, the restoration of the *Rite of Christian Initiation of Adults* provides a major focus for the way Lent is celebrated. Liturgical celebrations during Lent include the Rite of Sending and the Rite of Election on the first Sunday of Lent and the Scrutinies on the third, fourth and fifth Sundays. The Mass of the Lord's Supper on Holy Thursday, with the washing of feet ceremony, is rich with significance for loving service. Catechumens and candidates for full communion are in a period of repentance, reconciliation and prayerful expectation (Enlightenment and Purification) during Lent.

While the traditional Lenten practices of prayer, fasting and almsgiving are still important, emphasis now also includes the preparation of the "elect" for their baptism through prayerful consideration of sin, repentance, conversion and reconciliation. Through the catechumens, we all are called to re-discover and re-examine the significance of our own baptisms and the ways God is calling us all to new life.

A Time of Prayer and Fasting

Jesus based his life and ministry on prayer: the foundation of our Lenten discipline. Perhaps no other discipline is as difficult for us today as finding time to pray in the midst of schedules already crammed with obligations. Making the time takes serious effort, patience, and support from other Christians.

Lent can be a time to dedicate ourselves to that effort. Lent can be a time when we go apart, each alone, to pray in silence, as well as a time when we come together with other Christians to share our prayer.

Jesus is our model in fasting and self-denial, too. His first expression of Sonship after his baptism was his willingness to fast for 40 days, sustained by God's word alone. All Christians promise to place the love of God above every other love. Part of the purpose of Lenten self-denial is to reveal to us gently how far our hearts may be from keeping that promise.

Fasting helps us come to know what really matters to us. As we fast, often God opens our hearts to alms-giving, another traditional Lenten discipline. When we give to the poor what we would have spent on ourselves, we live life more abundantly.

The penitential tone of Lent is highlighted during worship service by using purple vestments and altar cloths. Some parishes, however, choose the natural color of unbleached linen or sackcloth.

Making Ready for the Feast

Many Christians undertake a Lenten rule giving guidelines for fasting and self-denial, as well as for praying, studying the Bible, and self-examination. Such rules are only means to the end, preparations for the Paschal feast. And, of course, our preparations for each Paschal feast now are only means to prepare us for the final banquet to which each of us is called by Jesus Christ.

Ancient legend said that Jesus would come again on an Easter night to call us to that final banquet. May we wait for him eagerly this Easter. May we come to Easter— and each day—with hearts prepared by discipline and hope for him who comes to fulfill every promise of spring: Jesus Christ our Lord.

Help! How do I plan this session?

How will I publicize this session?

_____

_____

How many people do I think might participate? _____

What are the ages of the participants?

_____

Where will we hold the session?

_____

Which recommended activities would work best with this particular group of participants? (Remember, we provide more activities than most groups can use in a single session. Pick a few that will work for your group.)

_____

_____

_____

_____

_____

_____

_____

_____

_____

Volunteers

to do	names	phone numbers
planning:		
preparation and set-up:		
activity leaders:		
clean-up:		

Session Plan

Gathering Prayer

Use the opening prayer for Ash Wednesday from the Sacramentary or read aloud the gospel for Ash Wednesday (Matthew 6:1-6, 16-18).

Key Idea

The Lenten season prepares Christians for the celebration of Easter.

Small Group Activity: Easter Garden

Materials

1 28" x 40" sheet of poster board
balloons
masking tape
newspaper
wallpaper or papier-mache paste
construction paper, assorted colors
tissue paper, assorted colors
scissors
glue
paint: spray, acrylic, tempera, or latex house paint
brush
shellac or varnish

Invite participants to prepare for Easter by constructing an Easter Garden, a small model of the garden where Jesus was laid to rest. The Easter Garden, constructed around an "empty tomb," can be set up on a table or floor. Possible locations for Easter Garden displays are chapel altars, unused doorways, tables inside the sanctuary, baptismal fonts, and outdoor locations.

Directions follow for constructing an "empty tomb" from papier-mache, but alternative construction methods include piling up stones or covering a wooden frame with crinkled grey or brown paper.

Directions to the participants: Blow up enough balloons to form a mound on the poster board 18"-24" high at its peak. Tape the balloons to the poster board and to each other.

Tear newspaper into 1" wide strips. Soak the strips in the paste and squeeze out the excess paste. Apply at least three layers of these papier-mache strips over the balloon mound, overlapping the strips and smoothing each layer down.

The mound will need to dry for three days. Make a door for the tomb by cutting many circles from newspaper, soaking the circles in paste, and layering the circles together.

Invite participants to make flowers from tissue paper and construction paper. Save these flowers to use as decorations for the Easter Garden on Holy Saturday.

When the papier-mache is dry, finish the Easter Garden by cutting a hole for the door, popping any remaining balloons, and removing the balloon scraps. Cover the opening with the door you have made. Paint with spray, acrylic, tempera, or latex house paint. When dry, apply a coat of shellac or varnish. Store the garden until Holy Saturday.

Sometime during Holy Saturday, set up the finished "empty tomb" on a green mat or florist's grass. Surround the finished "empty tomb" with flowers and plants. You may add an angel figure from a nativity set at the door of the tomb and place strips of white cloth inside the tomb.

Small Group Activity: Butterflies in Cocoons

Materials

> lightweight paper in bright colors:
>   construction, origami, gift wrap,
>   tissue, etc.
> scissors
> felt pens
> glue
> pipe cleaners
> trash bag ties
> cardboard tubes
> brown construction paper
> yarn
> tongue depressors
> knife

Invite participants to prepare soft paper butterflies that will be kept in paper cocoons and released on Easter Day. Encourage older participants to help younger ones with pattern-making and cutting.

Store the finished cocoons until Easter. On Easter Day, the butterflies can be released from the cocoons and either hung on heavy thread or attached to kite struts or balloon sticks and carried in procession.

Growing Together

Method One:

Use the pattern to trace a butterfly shape onto brightly colored paper. Cut out the butterfly. Decorate it with felt pens and cut-out paper shapes.

Fold a plastic trash bag tie or a pipe cleaner into a V-shape and glue it to the head of the butterfly. When dry, gently roll up the butterfly and place it in a cardboard tube or a tube made from brown construction paper. Cover a cardboard tube with tissue paper, tying each end with a length of yarn. Seal the ends of a construction paper tube with glue.

Method Two:

Use the pattern to trace two identical butterfly shapes on brightly colored paper. Cut out the butterflies. Decorate the butterflies with felt pens and cut-out paper shapes.

Glue the two butterflies to one tongue depressor, one butterfly on one side of the depressor and another butterfly on the other side. The tongue depressor becomes a handle.

Fold the wings of each butterfly outward. Add antennae and put into a cardboard tube cocoon, according to the instructions given in Method One.

Patterns for Butterflies in Cocoons

Growing Together

Key Idea

The experience of Jesus in the wilderness provides a model for our Lenten observances.

Small Group Activity: Story

Jesus Tells the Devil, "No!"

Jesus went into the desert so that he could spend time alone, listening and talking to God. Jesus didn't take any food to the desert. Forty days and 40 nights passed and Jesus had eaten nothing. He was very hungry.

The devil saw that Jesus was hungry and tired and alone in the desert. "Now is the time to trick Jesus," said the devil to himself. "He's so hungry, I'll bet he'll do anything for food. Now is the time to spoil God's plans for Jesus."

So the devil went to Jesus, who was alone and hungry in the desert. "Jesus," said the devil, "surely you must be hungry by now. If you're God's Son, why don't you change all these rocks into loaves of bread? Why, people everywhere would listen to you if they saw you change rocks to bread!"

Jesus raised his head and spoke. "No," said Jesus. "God's word says there is more to life than food. God wants people to follow me for love, not for bread."

The devil thought again. "Jesus," he said, "I have much power here on earth. If you bow down and worship me, I can give you all the people on earth as your followers."

"Never!" said Jesus. "God does not want unhappy slaves. I will worship God alone, and so will all who follow me."

The devil had one more trick up his sleeve. "Jesus," said the devil, "I'm beginning to wonder if you really know what God wants. In fact, I'm beginning to wonder if you really are God's Son.

"Prove it to me. Jump off the highest tower of the temple in Jerusalem. If you're God's Son, God won't let you get hurt. Maybe God will send angels to catch you," the devil added in a cruel voice.

Jesus stood and spoke again. "No. God's word says we must not put God to the test. I will obey my God." Jesus was tired and hungry, but as strong as a tower against the devil and all his tricks.

So the devil, in a rage, gave up and left Jesus there in the desert. God sent angels to Jesus, and they gave Jesus strength.

Small Group Activity: Bible Study (for older participants)

Materials

chalkboard and chalk or newsprint and markers

Bibles

Begin by asking participants, "What is the purpose of Lent?" Record all answers on chalkboard or newsprint.

Distribute Bibles to the participants. Ask for three volunteers, one to read Matthew 4:1-11; one to read Mark 1:9-13; and one to read Luke 4:1-13. Discuss:

- How do these stories differ?
- How do these stories agree?
- What purposes did Jesus' 40 days in the wilderness serve? (Record the answers to this question on chalkboard or newsprint.)
- What purposes did Jesus' fasting serve?
- What purposes did Jesus' temptations— and refusals to submit to temptations— serve?
- What did Jesus give up when he refused each temptation?
- What other 40-day or 40-year periods of special significance are mentioned in scripture?
  — Which, if any, also portray a cleansing or renewing time of preparation before something new comes into being?
- How can Jesus' time in the wilderness serve as a model for our Lenten observances?

Divide the participants into small groups of four or five participants each. Ask each group to discuss these two questions:

- What do you value from your past experiences during Lent?
- In what new ways do you want to observe Lent this year?

Key Idea

Three biblical stories from John's gospel (the woman at the well, the man born blind and the raising of Lazarus) are proclaimed on the Scrutiny Sundays each year in parishes where catechumens are present. In this section, we offer discussion starters especially suited for younger participants.

Small Group Activity: Exploring "The Woman at the Well"

Materials

pitcher of water

cups

Pour small cups of water for those who want them. Ask:

- When do we especially want a cup of cold water to drink?

Growing Together

- When do we like to splash or play in water?
- On what kinds of days do we like to watch water coming down like rain?

Explain that Jesus once longed for a cold cup of water himself—as they can hear in today's story. Then read aloud John 4:7-10, 25-26, 28-30, 39-40.

Remind children of times when they feel thirsty and want water to drink. Discuss:
- When we see others thirsty, what do we want to do for them?

Explain:
- Hearing good news about Jesus can feel as good as drinking a cool glass of water when you are very, very thirsty.
- The Samaritan people were very glad when the woman told them the good news that Jesus was the one God had sent to them.
- What good news about Jesus do we know?
- What good news about Jesus can we share?
- How can we share good news about Jesus with others?

Small Group Activity: Exploring "The Man Born Blind"

Ask:
- If we could ask Jesus to change just one thing in our lives, what would we ask?

Encourage many different answers to this question. Be careful to create an accepting atmosphere, especially when children give their answers.

For example, children may well wish that their baby brothers or sisters would not live with them anymore. We can accept the children's remarks as accurate statements of their feelings, without expressing either approval or disapproval. *Example:*
- You wish that you didn't have a baby brother in your family.

Invite participants to hear the story of a big change in someone's life. Then read aloud John 9:1-11.

Discuss:
- What did Jesus change for the man in today's story?

Explain:
- God's power can change our lives and change the world we live in.
- One way God's power can change lives is when *we* make changes in our lives and in our world.
- What are some ways we can make changes in our lives?

Small Group Activity: Exploring "The Raising of Lazarus"

Materials

drawing paper and crayons or felt pens

Discuss:
- What happens when someone dies?
- How do we feel about death or dying?
- What do we wish we knew about death or dying?
- What questions do we have about death or dying?

Be especially careful to affirm the importance of children's questions. Many of the questions children have about death are questions that perplexed the greatest thinkers our world has known.

Then read aloud John 11:1-3, 17, 20-29, 32-44. Discuss:
- What did Jesus do for Lazarus?
- We call what Jesus did *resurrection*. This word means giving life after death.
- The Bible tells us that Jesus gave Lazarus life after death.
- The Bible tells us that God gave Jesus life after death.
- The Bible also tells us that God will give each one of us new life after death.
- There's still a lot that we don't know about death or resurrection. We don't know what it will be like to die. We don't know exactly what new life with God will be like. We still have many, many questions about death and life after death. *(Invite children to think of questions they have about resurrection and life after death.)*

Invite children to draw pictures about resurrection or life after death. They can draw pictures from today's gospel, or pictures that show some of their own questions or understanding of life after death.

Key Idea

Christians are called to observe Lent through discipline and self-denial.

Small Group Activity: Lenten Calendars

Materials

chalkboard and chalk or newsprint
and markers
8 1/2" x 11" paper, 1 sheet per
participant
pencils
rulers
felt pens

Invite participants to make Lenten Calendars to use as guidelines for Lenten observances.

Before the session use the blank calendar provided here to prepare two Lenten calendars, each on a sheet of 8-1/2" x 11" paper. Write a number in each square, following the calendar for this current year.

Growing Together

Begin the first calendar with Ash Wednesday and include the first 20 days of Lent. (Remember that Sundays are feast days and are not counted in the 40 days of Lent.) The second calendar will include the last 20 days of Lent.

Ask the participants to brainstorm ways to observe Lent. Ask for specific ideas:

- What ways can we encourage self-examination and repentance?
- What ways can we encourage prayer?
- What ways can we encourage fasting and self-denial?
- What ways can we encourage almsgiving?
- What ideas could we give to encourage reading and meditating on God's word?

Record all ideas on chalkboard or newsprint. Ask participants to divide into two groups and distribute the prepared Lenten calendars, each group preparing a calendar for 20 days of Lent.

Have each group fill each box on the calendar with one idea for a Lenten observance. Provide felt pens for decorating the finished calendars.

When the groups have completed the project, make copies of the two calendars for each participant. If a copy machine is not available, you may wish to post the calendars and have participants write down the suggestions week by week or print each week's suggestions in your Sunday bulletins. Encourage the participants to consult the calendar suggestions daily as an aid to keeping a holy Lent.

Leader's Resources: Outreach

- Almsgiving is important throughout the year, but especially during Lent. Invite households to prayerfully consider what portion of their income they will share with the poor and needy during Lent. Contact Catholic Relief Services (*www.catholicrelief.org* or 1-800-736-3467) for their popular and traditional "Operation Rice Bowl" family money collection activity or for other creative ideas for prayerful stewardship.

Leader's Tip

Stories can lead to effective discussions with younger participants. Possible questions for this story include:

- Who do you think is the most important person in this story? Why?
- From this story, what did you find out about Jesus that you did not already know? What did you find out about the devil?

- What are the three things the devil tempted Jesus to do?
- How would you feel if the devil offered you these things?

- What do Jesus' answers tell you about his relationship with God?
- What kind of strength do you think the angels gave to Jesus?

Be sure to accept all answers, especially those that may differ from your own opinions.

LENTEN CALENDAR

MONTH: _____ YEAR: _____

SUNDAY	MONDAY	TUESDAY	WEDNESDAY	THURSDAY	FRIDAY	SATURDAY
FEAST DAY						
FEAST DAY						
FEAST DAY						
FEAST DAY						
FEAST DAY						

Growing Together

- Lent is a good time to remember those in the parish who are homebound, elderly, sick or suffering. Invite households to adopt one such member in the parish to help with errands or transportation. Many homebound people now use e-mail. Households can use this medium to send even daily messages of fellowship and support.

- Ask families to create banners or posters welcoming into the parish those who are preparing for initiation this Easter. These works of art can be presented to catechumens and candidates for full communion on Holy Saturday prior to the Easter Vigil.

Small Group Activity: Following Jesus Game

Invite participants to play a discipleship game. Have the participants sit in a circle. Begin the game by saying, "I am going to follow Jesus, and I will follow him by *(name an activity)*." You might choose an answer from traditional Lenten observances, such as *reading the Bible* or *fasting*.

Have the next player repeat the sentence, first naming your activity, and then adding a second activity. Play continues in this fashion until a player cannot name all the activities in order. This player may start the second game.

Be sure to accept all answers, especially those of younger participants. If necessary, modify this game for very young participants by omitting the repetitions.

Small Group Activity: Discussion (for older participants)
Materials

> copies of the Commandment Study Sheet, found at the end of this activity

Ask several volunteers to read aloud the Ten Commandments from the Decalogue. (Use copies of the *Catechism* or Bible.) Ask the participants to divide into 10 study groups, each group to study one of the Ten Commandments using the Commandment Study Sheet.

Commandment Study Sheet

1. What stories from the Bible can you recall in which this commandment was obeyed?

2. What stories from the Bible can you recall in which this commandment was disobeyed?

3. What examples from everyday life show people obeying this commandment?

4. What examples from everyday life show people disobeying this commandment?

5. Why do you think God gave this commandment to us?

6. How would you state this commandment in positive terms today?

Allow 15 minutes for work, then reassemble the group. Ask each study group to report on its findings and discuss:

● Which commandment do you think is most important to God's people today? Why?

● Which commandment do you think is least obeyed among God's people today? Why?

● Do you think the Ten Commandments are sufficient guidelines for God's people today? Why or why not?

● Do you think Jesus' teachings complement or contradict the Ten Commandments? Why?

● If you kept all the Ten Commandments perfectly, do you think you would continue to grow closer to God? Why or why not?

Key Idea

Prayer provides the foundation of our Lenten discipline.

Small Group Activity: Way of the Cross

Invite the participants to pray the Way of the Cross, a traditional Lenten devotion designed to tell the Passion story through a set of readings and prayers. The devotion grew from the customs of pilgrims who traveled to Jerusalem and offered prayers in the city at places associated with Jesus' Passion.

Any traditional Way of the Cross devotional could work for this activity, or participants could invent their own.

Suggestions:

● Invite participants to perform short skits at each station, portraying the scene commemorated.

● Invite participants to write their own meditations for each station.

● Invite participants to make collages, posters, sculptures, etc. to represent each station. (For example, an ornate chair would be a good marker for Station 1, a cross for Station 5 or a pair of dice for Station 10.)

Following the devotions at the last Station, ask the participants to pray together The Lord's Prayer.

Growing Together

Large Group Activity: Thanking Jesus

Materials

> chalkboard and chalk or newsprint and markers

Have the participants work together to write a litany of thanksgiving to Jesus. Write on the chalkboard or newsprint:

Jesus, I know you love me because only someone who loves me would...

Divide the participants into pairs, encouraging older participants to pair with younger participants. Ask each pair to decide on an ending to the sentence and to write it on the chalkboard or newsprint.

Ask the participants to gather around the chalkboard or newsprint. Ask the first participant to read the sentence including the first ending from the chalkboard or newsprint. Ask the group to respond to the reading by saying, "Thank you, Jesus," in unison.

Have the participants continue reading and responding until all the endings have been read. Then finish the litany by praying:

Jesus, thank you for the love you have shown to each one of us. Help us to love others as you love us in the days of Lent and ever after. *Amen*.

Small Group Activity: Rule Discovery (for older participants)

Materials

> paper
> pens or pencils
> chalkboard and chalk or newsprint and markers

Note: This activity invites participants to consider a rule of prayer for Lent. Please note that a rule must not be thought of as a set of actions by which Christians can earn favor from God. A Christian rule is a *response* to the saving love of God given to us in Jesus Christ.

Distribute paper and pencils. Ask participants to list how they manage their time—daily, weekly, or monthly—in the following areas (list these on chalkboard or newsprint):

- sleeping
- working
- eating
- driving
- time with family
- recreation
- reading
- television
- prayer
- reading the Bible
- prayer time with other Christians

Allow 10 minutes for work. Then ask the participants to consider the idea that these papers represent our current "rules"—our habits, our regular ways with time and prayer.

Explain:

- Many of us have heard of monastic Rules, such as the Rule of St. Benedict.
- The English word **rule** is based on the Latin word **regula**, related to our word **regular**. It describes what we regularly do in an ordinary day, week or year.
- We can consider the way we use our time already to be our current "rule."

Discuss:

- What part of your rule gives you the most satisfaction?
- What part of your rule do you wish you could change?
- What obstacles stand in the way of changes we want to make?
- What possible solutions can you imagine for your own obstacles?

Ask participants to take another 10 minutes to write down new rules that represent the participants' desires for change.

Key Idea

The Lenten season is marked by several traditional customs, including special Lenten foods and devotions.

Small Group Activity: Pretzels

Materials

2 packages dry yeast
1-1/2 cups warm water
4-5 cups flour
1 tablespoon sugar
1 teaspoon salt
coarse salt

Other materials:

measuring cup
bowl
mixing spoon
8-10 quart pot
slotted spoon
cookie sheet
oven

One story about the origin of pretzels tells that bakers made the shapes—representing arms crossed in prayer—to give interest to plain Lenten food. Another story says that monks made the shapes as Lenten rewards for students. The twisted shapes, boiled and baked, still make fine Lenten treats today.

Directions to the participants: Soak the yeast in 1/4 cup warm water for five minutes. Add the remaining water and beat in 4 cups of the flour, the sugar, and the salt. Add as much of the remaining flour as necessary to make a dough that is firm enough to be kneaded, but is still soft.

Knead the dough for 10 minutes. Let rise in a warm spot for 45 minutes. Punch down the dough. Divide the dough into

24 small pieces. Roll each piece into a rope. Twist each rope into a pretzel shape.

Bring 6 to 8 quarts of water to a boil. Drop in the pretzels, no more than two at a time. The pretzels will first sink and then rise to the top of the pot. When a pretzel rises, flip it over and boil it 15 seconds on the second side. Then remove the pretzel with a slotted spoon and place the pretzel on a cookie sheet. Continue for the other pretzels.

Sprinkle the boiled pretzels with coarse salt. Bake at 425 degrees for 12-15 minutes. Eat while still warm.

▶ Small Group Activity: Lenten Recipe Book

Materials

  blank white paper, each sheet punched
    with 3 holes
  pens
  pencils
  felt pens
  poster board for a sign
  reinforcements
  3-ring binder
  Optional:
  construction paper
  yarn

Before the session invite participants to bring recipes to be compiled in a Lenten Recipe Book for your parish to use as a resource.

Especially appropriate are:
- meatless recipes
- recipes that use fish
- recipes that are low-cost
- traditional Lenten recipes from other cultures

You may wish to keep the finished recipe book on display during the Lenten season or place it in your parish library. If you decide to make copies of the book, make sure all pictures are drawn with black felt pens only, to permit clear reproduction.

Set up a center where participants can take turns working on the book. Provide a table, chairs, blank white paper, pens and pencils, and felt pens. Post a sign that reads: *Have a favorite Lenten recipe? Write it down for the parish to share.*

Invite younger participants to decorate the written recipes with pictures or decorative borders. Reinforce the holes of the written recipes and place them in a three-ring binder.

If you have access to a copier and wish to make copies of the book at the session, ask younger participants to make covers for the books from construction paper. Bind the books by stringing yarn through the holes in the paper.

Small Group Activity: Palm Crosses

Materials

18" palm fronds, 1 per participant

Invite participants to make palm crosses for use in your Palm Sunday service.

Directions to participants: Hold the palm frond horizontally. Fold the right half straight up from the center to form a right angle.

Fold the top strip of the frond toward the back and down, up and over again, to form a square as you look at it from the back. It will still be a right angle.

Bring the left strip forward and fold it over the center toward the right. Then bend it away from you and pull it through the square at the back, all the way. This is the locking step.

Bend the top strip forward and put the end through the center square to make a shaft of desired length.

Bend the left strip backward and put it through the back square. This makes the left cross-bar. Adjust it in proportion to the upright of the cross.

Fold the right strip to the back and put it through the back square to fasten it.

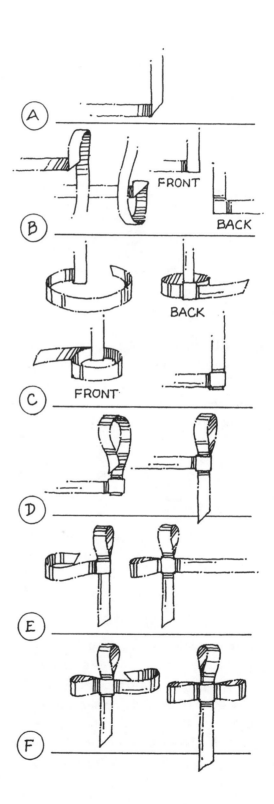

Growing Together

Large Group Activity: Ojos De Dios

Materials

> sticks or dowels
> yarn in various colors
> glue
> scissors
> felt markers

Invite the participants to make Mexican crosses, called Ojos de Dios (God's Eyes), for Lent. The making of Ojos de Dios is a traditional craft of the Huichol Indians of northwest Mexico.

Begin by having the participants go on a walk to gather sticks. If weather and location make this unfeasible, gather the sticks yourself **before the session**, looking for a variety of lengths and thicknesses. Or you may provide dowels at the session.

Directions to the participants: Pick two sticks to use in making a cross. Form a cross with the sticks and glue them at the intersection. Now cut a length of yarn. Tie the yarn to one stick at the point where the two sticks cross. Weave the yarn over and under the sticks in a circle around the point where the two sticks cross.

Continue weaving in a circle around the cross point. Use several colors to make a design that pleases you. The wrapping may continue to the outer ends of the sticks or may stop several inches in from the ends. If it stops in from the ends, wrap the exposed sticks with yarn or color the ends of the sticks with a felt marker matching the yarn that was last wrapped.

Participants may wish to carry the crosses in procession at mass or to take them home.

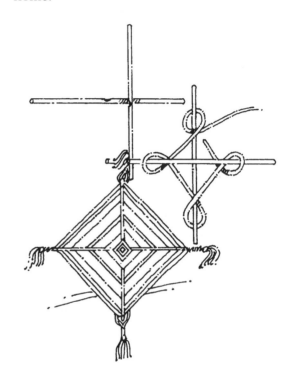

 Leader's Resources: Multicultural Issues

- Teach and sing one of the popular "Senor, Ten Piedad" ("Lord, have mercy") penitential songs. Some composers include Alejandro Meja, Orlando Alturas and the versions found in Misa Popular or Misa Panamericana.

● Read aloud *The Legend of the Bluebonnet* by Tomie dePaola (New York: G.P. Putnam's Sons, 1983) and encourage discussion among family members. This story is about the courage and sacrifice of a young Comanche girl and the forgiveness that follows her selfless action—a perfect Lenten story.

 ## Closing Prayer

Gather the parish family into a prayer circle (several circles if the group is large). Sing together one or more verses of the American spiritual "Were you there when they crucified my Lord?" Pray together in one of the following ways:

● Pass a cross or crucifix around the circle. As each person receives it, he or she may hold it and audibly or silently express thanks to Jesus for who he is or what he has done.

● Place a cross or crucifix in the center of the circle. Suggest that anyone who wishes may extend a hand or both hands toward the cross in an act of commitment, praying for grace to follow a specific Lenten rule or giving thanks for Jesus' life.

Easter

Introduction and Information

Easter is both a feast and a season—the Great Fifty Days—beginning with the Easter Vigil and lasting until Pentecost. Our Christian ancestors delighted in making extravagant claims for Easter; it was the queen of feasts and the solemnity of solemnities. The 50 days were a sabbath of sabbaths—seven weeks of seven days, symbolic of eternity itself.

Easter is the day and the season for endless rejoicing. The Council of Nicea forbade kneeling or fasting during Easter, prohibitions that can serve us well today. We need to become as devout in our festivities during the Great Fifty Days as we are in our austerities during Lent.

Providing a Model of Easter Festivity

The Christian community faces a curious situation during the Easter season: the secular world provides little competition, compared to the commercialism of the Christmas season, but it also provides little support for 50 days of celebration. In our households and in our parishes, we must support each other, thus providing the model of Easter festivity for the rest of society.

We can begin by recovering some of the Easter traditions of our Christian heritage. Visiting was one such tradition. Priests in some countries visited parishioners' homes during the Easter season. The priests would bless the homes, and the parishioners would share Easter food with the priests.

Parishioners paid visits, too, to the shut-ins of their communities. Such visits are even more appropriate today when the number of institutionalized members of our communities has grown so much. Nursing home residents are obvious—and important—examples, but we can also extend our visiting to include prisoners, homeless families in shelters, and victims of family violence in safe houses.

Easter Foods

We might bring special foods on our Easter visits. In many countries, Christian communities have developed Easter foods that have been served for generations, such as sweet white cheeses or ham with parsley. The most common Easter foods are special breads, such as the Russian kulich—rich in eggs, butter, and sugar.

Passover

Perhaps the ubiquity of Easter bread reflects the ancestry of our Easter celebrations in the Jewish Passover, a feast marked by the consumption of unleavened bread. Easter is the Church's Passover feast, a time of celebration for God's mighty acts of salvation.

Passover is celebrated by an annual retelling of the story of God's redemption. This Passover act finds its counterpart in the Easter liturgy, when we gather in the night to hear of God's creation, redemption and sanctification of God's people.

In the Jewish Seder and at the Church's Easter Vigil, we also hear how God brought the Israelites through water to their salvation. This Passover theme is underscored in the Easter liturgy, which is also the Church's primary baptismal liturgy.

A Baptismal Season

The Neophytes (the newly baptized) experience the sacraments of Easter as the basis for their understanding of the period of Mystagogy that includes the fifty days of Easter. New life, through Baptism, Confirmation and Eucharist, is celebrated not only on Easter Sunday but throughout the Easter Season.

All these stories and rites, told and enacted in the Church's liturgy, should only be the beginning of our Easter stories. In one sense, the history of our Church could be summed up in the words of the disciples as they told their story to Thomas: "We have seen the Lord!" (John 20:25b)

This is the day and the season for our witness to the Risen Lord. We must speak to those growing up in a perilous age, to those facing the end of their lives or other endings, to those imprisoned by guilt or fear or violence, and to all who struggle to be faithful to the mystery of the gospel.

The Lord is risen. He is risen indeed. This is our day of joy and our season of endless victory. Alleluia!

Help! How do I plan this session?

How will I publicize this session?

_____

_____

How many people do I think might participate? _____

What are the ages of the participants?

_____

Where will we hold the session?

_____

Which recommended activities would work best with this particular group of participants? (Remember, we provide more activities than most groups can use in a single session. Pick a few that will work for your group.)

_____

_____

_____

_____

_____

_____

_____

_____

Volunteers

to do	names	phone numbers
planning:		
preparation and set-up:		
activity leaders:		
clean-up:		

Growing Together

Session Plan

Gathering Prayer

Sing an Easter hymn or proclaim the gospel for Easter Sunday (John 20:1-9).

Key Idea

Easter names both a day and a season. The celebration of Easter should extend for a full 50 days.

Small Group Activity: Easter Calendars

Materials

> large sheets of newsprint
> felt pens or pencils
> *Optional:*
> chalkboard and chalk

Invite participants to make Easter Calendars to use as reminders to celebrate the full 50 days of Easter. **Before the session** make enough copies of the calendar provided at the end of this lesson for each participant to have one.

Begin by asking participants to brainstorm ways to celebrate days in the Easter season—ordinary days as well as special feasts, such as Ascension. If ideas are slow in coming, ask these or similar questions:

- What scripture passages are good to hear during Easter?
- What activities could help your household feel the joy of Easter?
- What songs are good to sing during Easter?

Record all suggestions on chalkboard or newsprint. Suggestions you might add include:

- For the Monday after Easter, plan a traditional "Easter Fools" day—to celebrate the trick Jesus played on the devil by rising from the dead. (This was a traditional European practice.)
- Praise God for the waters of salvation! Have a late spring picnic by a country stream or a city fountain.
- On the Fourth Sunday after Easter, Good Shepherd Sunday, read Psalm 23.
- Thank Jesus for witnesses to his risen life. Begin with the women Jesus chose as his very first witnesses.
- On the Feast of Ascension, have a kite-flying celebration.

If participants suggest activities suitable for the entire parish family gathered together, consider forming a committee to plan a time for the activity.

Then invite each participant to make an Easter Calendar. Ask older participants to pair with younger participants for this project.

Directions to participants: Write a number in each square, following the calendar for this current year. Fill in each box on the calendar with one idea for an Easter celebration.

Provide felt pens for decorating the finished calendars. Encourage the participants to take home their calendars to use during the whole Easter season.

▶ Small Group Activity: Easter Prayer Books

Materials

> 8 1/2" x 11" white paper
> 9" x 12" construction paper in assorted colors
> yarn
> scissors
> glue
> felt pens
> hole punches

Invite participants to make prayer books suitable for individual or family use during Easter. We suggest topics for participants to use in writing their own prayers, but keep missals available, too, for participants to use if they wish to include such ancient prayers as the Easter Proclamation (the Exsultet) or Psalm 118:1-2, 16, 17, 22-23.

At the session distribute paper, construction paper, hole punches, yarn, scissors, glue and felt pens. Invite participants to work together to write Easter prayers, or to copy prayers from traditional sources. Participants could choose to write prayers about:new life, signs of nature awakening in the spring, Jesus as our hope and our friend, etc. Small groups could exchange their prayers with other groups, too.

Invite each participant to mount the copies on white paper, to decorate these pages, and to bind them into a book with construction paper and yarn.

Set the books aside for the closing prayer activity.

Growing Together

Small Group Activity: Easter Tree

Materials

> either an outdoor bush or tree *or* a branch stuck in a pot of rocks
> chalkboard and chalk or newsprint and marker
> clean Styrofoam meat or vegetable trays or Styrofoam picnic plates
> scissors
> glue
> collage materials: felt, sequins, glitter, rickrack, buttons, foil, etc.
> narrow ribbon (preferably satin)

Invite participants to decorate an Easter tree. Choose a bush or tree outside or anchor a bare branch in a pot of rocks. Ask participants to make decorations for the tree using Easter symbols. (See the Patterns for Easter Symbols, p. 57.)

Begin by asking participants to brainstorm a list of Easter symbols. Encourage inventing new symbols as well as recalling such traditional ones as:

- eggs
- lambs
- pomegranates
- butterflies
- lilies

Divide participants into small groups of four or five. Ask each small group to produce six decorations for the Easter tree. These may be cut from Styrofoam (using patterns from this book) or cut free hand and decorated with collage materials.

The ornaments can be tied to the tree with narrow ribbon. You might want to invite participants to sing Easter hymns while decorating the tree.

Encourage members of your parish family to add new decorations to the tree each Sunday of the Easter season.

Leader's Tip

Be sure to follow through on Lenten preparations for Easter, especially:

- releasing the butterflies from their cocoons (p. 33)
- surrounding the Easter Garden (p. 32) with plants
- bringing out the Alleluia Poster (p. 25) with noise and merriment—bells or kazoos or rhythm band instruments—and placing the poster in a place of honor during Easter. Participants can then sing some of the different "Alleluia" versions suggested in the Mardi Gras session

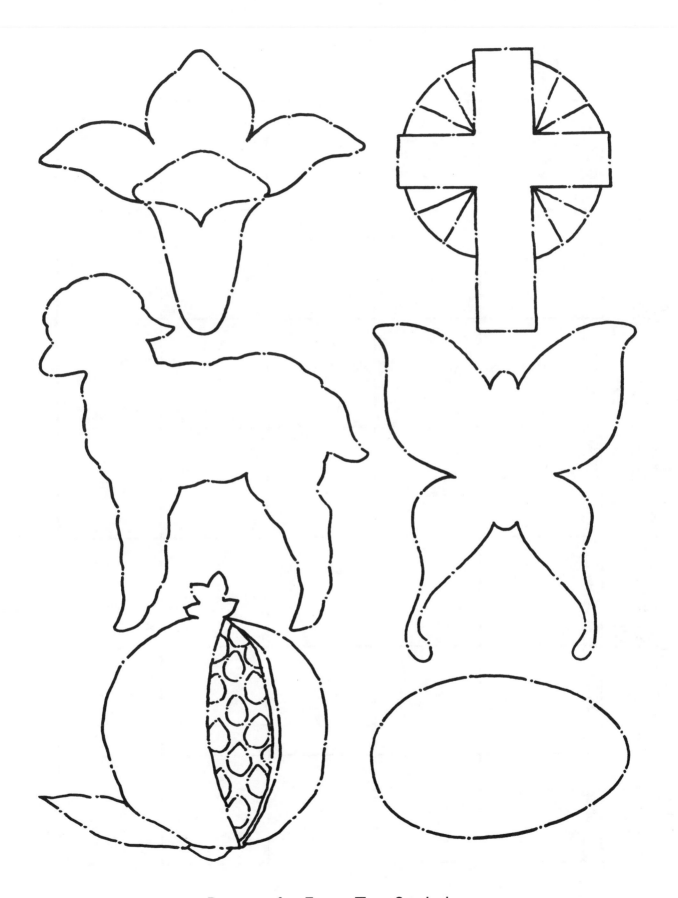

Patterns for Easter Tree Symbols

EASTER CALENDAR

MONTH: _____ YEAR: _____

SUNDAY	MONDAY	TUESDAY	WEDNESDAY	THURSDAY	FRIDAY	SATURDAY

Key Idea

Visiting shut-ins is a traditional activity of the Easter Season. Participants can make cards to spread the joy of the Easter season.

Large Group Activity: Easter Cards

Materials

chalkboard and chalk or newsprint and marker

white paper

construction paper

felt pens

crayons

scissors

glue

newspapers

construction paper

collage materials (cotton, felt, sequins, glitter, ribbon, yarn, etc.)

chalk

hair spray

potatoes

knives

stamp pads

Invite participants to make Easter greeting cards to spread the joyous news of the resurrection of Jesus Christ. Begin by asking participants to brainstorm appropriate messages. Record all suggestions on chalk-board or newsprint. If ideas are slow in coming, ask these or similar questions:

- How can we tell the Easter story in only a few words?
- What songs do you like to hear on Easter day?
- Why do we celebrate Easter?

Ask each participant to make a card, decorating it and writing a message on it. Older participants can help young ones write their messages.

Make available a variety of materials, including both white paper and construction paper as card stock. (If you like, provide cardboard patterns, using Patterns for Easter Symbols, p. 57.)

Encourage creativity. A card might be cut in the shape of an Easter symbol, or a traditional folded card could be decorated with:

- Easter symbols drawn in felt pens or crayons
- symbols cut and glued from newspaper or construction paper
- collage symbols made from cotton, felt, sequins, glitter, ribbon, yarn, etc.
- symbols drawn in chalk on colored construction paper and fixed with hair spray
- symbols carved in a potato half and stamped, first on a stamp pad, then on the cards

Send the cards home with participants to be mailed to friends.

Growing Together

Large Group Activity: "You Were There" Postcards

Materials

9" x 6" sheets of construction paper, 1 per participant

felt pens and crayons

Read aloud to the group the Easter story as it is written in Matthew 28:1-9.

Directions to participants: Pretend that you were with the women who found the tomb empty on the first Easter morning. How will you tell another person this good news? Make a postcard or greeting card and write a message to a friend, writing as if you were one of those first witnesses. Sign your card with your real name.

Pass the finished cards around for everyone to enjoy. Afterward ask participants if they wish to take their cards home, leave the cards on display at your parish, or send them to the shut-ins of your community.

If you send the cards, you might include a letter explaining that they were made as a learning activity at your parish and that you are sending them as a way of sharing your joy that Jesus is risen.

Leader's Tip

The most effective service projects further the work that your parish already does. No church family can "do it all." Focus your efforts on supporting the ongoing ministries of your parish.

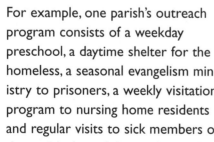

For example, one parish's outreach program consists of a weekday preschool, a daytime shelter for the homeless, a seasonal evangelism ministry to prisoners, a weekly visitation program to nursing home residents and regular visits to sick members of the parish. Any of these ministries would provide appropriate recipients of Easter greetings and visits.

Small Group Activity: Easter Wheat

Materials

inexpensive baskets or pots

plastic wrap for lining baskets

potting soil

wheat seeds (available as whole wheat at natural foods stores)

spray bottles of water

plastic bags

Invite participants to make gifts of Easter Wheat to take on Easter visits. The European custom of growing wheat at Easter, as a symbol of Jesus' death and resurrection, is finding new popularity in our own times. You can use newly sprouted wheat grass as a living Easter basket or a table decoration. An appropriate contemporary hymn to accompany making the project would be "Now the Green Blade Riseth."

Directions to participants: Take a pot or basket (lined with plastic wrap) and fill it almost to the top with soil. Sprinkle a thick pinch of wheat seeds over the surface of the soil. Carefully water the soil with a spray bottle and put the watered pot or basket in a plastic bag. Keep in a warm place and check daily for sprouting. When sprouts appear, remove from the bag and put in a sunny location. You'll have new green grass in 7-14 days.

Key Idea

Our Easter feast is a Paschal feast, rooted in the Jewish Passover.

Small Group Activity: Paschal Questions and Answers

Materials

copies of the Paschal Talk, below

The Jewish liturgy of Passover—a family liturgy—takes its structure from a natural family act: children asking questions of elders. Invite participants to gather into mixed-age groups of 10-12 participants each for questions and answers about our own Paschal feast.

Ask one participant in each group to serve as leader. Give each leader a copy of the Paschal Discussion Sheet (below).

Allow 20-30 minutes for discussion. Then reconvene the group and ask each participant to finish this sentence: ***What I like best about Easter is...***

Paschal Talk

1. How do we celebrate Easter?

2. Why do you think we light a candle at the Easter vigil?

3. Why do we unveil the crosses in our church at Easter and fill the church with flowers?

4. What stories do we hear at Easter and why?

5. Why do you think we baptize people at Easter?

6. Why do you think we sing and say ***alleluia*** at Easter?

7. Why do you think we ring bells at Easter?

8. Why do you think we hunt for eggs at Easter?

Growing Together

▶ Small Group Activity: Paschal Banner

Materials

    chalkboard and chalk or newsprint
      and marker
    scissors
    felt
    burlap, at least 24" x 48"
    1/4" dowel to attach to the upper
      edge of the banner
    string

Note: Extensive, easily adaptable instructions for making banners may be found in *Growing Together: Six Intergenerational Celebrations, Volume I, Fall & Winter*.

Ask participants to begin by thinking of names for Easter. Encourage participants who know the name of Easter in languages other than English to contribute these names. You also might borrow dictionaries of other languages from a library. These names will show the link between Passover and Easter in other languages.

Encourage participants to make up their own names, too; egg day, butterfly day, or chocolate day are names you may hear. Record all suggestions on chalkboard or newsprint.

Invite participants to make a banner of names for Easter. Have participants cut felt letters for these names to glue onto the length of burlap. Non-spelling participants may prefer to cut out Easter symbols for the banner. (See Patterns for Easter Symbols, p. 57.) Ask one participant to make large letters for the name *Easter* to run down the vertical length of the banner.

Attach the dowel with glue to the upper edge of the banner. Attach string to the dowel. Hang up the banner and discuss:

- What is your favorite name for Easter? Why?
- Easter and Passover, the Jewish feast that celebrates the Israelites' escape from slavery in Egypt, have the same name in many languages. Why do you think this is so?
- How do you think God frees people by raising Jesus from the dead?
- In what ways are you aware of God's freeing power in your life? in the life of someone you know?

Leader's Resources: Multicultural Issues

- Two good videos for this season would be "Phos: the Light" and "Baptism: Sacrament of Belonging," both available from St. Anthony Press and Franciscan Communications. "Phos" is a 19-minute video that explores the meaning of sorrow and forgiveness in the life of a young Greek boy. It is presented within the context of the Easter Vigil, in Greek with English sub-titles. "Baptism" is a 15-minute video classic, presenting a young orphaned Mexico boy who is welcomed and given a new life. Allow time for discussion after either or both videos.

- Good hymns to sing would include "This Little Light of Mine," a traditional African-American spiritual; "Jesu Tawa Pano" by Patrick Matsikenyiri, a simple melody that proclaims "Jesus, we are here, we are here for you" in the Zimbabwe language and in English; and "Resucito" by Kiko Arguello, a popular Easter hymn in Spanish proclaiming, "He lives!"

▶ Small Group Activity: Passover Prayer (for older participants)

Materials

Bibles
newsprint and markers
masking tape

Ask the group to begin by thinking of words that define the word *redemption*. Write all suggestions on newsprint. Younger members of the group may find it easier to give definitions for other words that suggest redemption, such as *freedom* or *saving*.

Divide into small groups of four or five participants. Ask the small groups to think of as many of God's acts of redemption as possible. Groups may draw on stories from the Bible or from participants' lives as examples.

Ask each group to record its thoughts; provide markers, masking tape, and several sheets of newsprint to each group. Allow 15 minutes for work.

Then reconvene the group, taping the posters up on a wall. Have the group gather into a circle. Ask the participants to join you in a traditional Passover thanksgiving for God's mighty acts of redemption.

The actual prayers should arise from the group's own research. This model only provides an example of the structure used:

Growing Together

Participant #1:

If the Lord had brought us out of Egypt, it would have been more than enough.

Participant #2:

If the Lord had brought us out of Egypt and had not brought us to the promised land, it would have been more than enough.

Participant #3:

If the Lord had brought us to the promised land and had not sent us the prophets, it would have been more than enough.

Participant #4:

If the Lord had sent us the prophets and had not come to us in Jesus, it would have been more than enough.

Participant #5:

If the Lord had come to us in Jesus and had not called us to be his disciples, it would have been more than enough.

Be prepared to end the round of prayer with a final thanksgiving, perhaps using this closing:

If the Lord had called us together as a family at *(name your parish)*, it would have been more than enough.

Key Idea

God saved the Israelites by leading them through the Red Sea on dry land. This Passover theme of water as a symbol of salvation is preserved in the liturgy of Easter, the Church's primary baptismal feast.

Small Group Activity: Baptismal Skits

Materials

Bibles

Invite the participants to improvise 5 minute skits from stories of baptisms in the Bible. Divide the participants into five groups. Two of the groups can have only two participants each. The other groups can accommodate as many participants as are needed.

Assign each group one of these stories:
- Luke 3:1-15 (many participants)
- Matthew 3:13-17 (two participants)
- Acts 2:1-17, 32-42 (many participants)
- Acts 8:26-40 (two participants)
- Acts 9:1-18 (many participants)

Give the groups 15 minutes to prepare the skits. Then have each group present its skit to the other participants.

Discuss:

● What led to the baptisms in each one of these situations?

● What effect did baptism seem to have on the individuals?

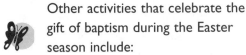

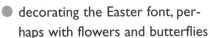

Leader's Tip

Other activities that celebrate the gift of baptism during the Easter season include:

● decorating the Easter font, perhaps with flowers and butterflies

● making and decorating candles as Easter or baptismal gifts

● water play—warm weather and old clothes needed!—with spray bottles or pans of water

● inviting parents to tell children stories about the day they were baptized: why their names were chosen, who was present, how the child reacted to the waters, what kind of celebration followed, etc.

● inviting the newly baptized to come to this Easter session to get to know the families who prepared banners and good wishes for them. Ask the neophytes to describe and discuss the experience of coming into the Church and the impact that the parish community has had on their faith.

Small Group Activity: Bible Study (for older participants)

Materials

Bibles
copies of the Study Sheet, below
paper
pens or pencils

Invite the participants to study water as a sign of God's salvation. Divide into three groups. Ask one participant in each group to act as leader, one to act as reader, and a third to act as recorder. Give each leader a copy of the Study Sheet and give each recorder paper and a pen or pencil.

Assign each group one reading:

Group #1: Genesis 7:1–9:17
Group #2: Exodus 14:1–15:21
Group #3: Matthew 1:1-12; John 4:1-42

Allow the small groups 20 minutes to discuss these readings using the Study Sheet. Then reconvene the entire group and ask each group to give a very brief summary of its reading. Discuss:

● What similarities exist between these readings? What differences?

● Describe the scene and main ideas of each reading.

● What is the significance of water in each of these readings?

● If you could choose only one word to describe water in these readings, what word would you choose?

Growing Together

Study Sheet

1. Ask the reader to read the assigned reading aloud.

2. Discuss the reading with these questions:
   — What words would you use to describe water in this reading?
   — What is destroyed by water in this reading?
   — What is saved through water in this reading?
   — What promises of God are associated with water in this reading?

3. Ask the group to help the recorder summarize the main points of the discussion on a single sheet of paper.

Key Idea

Storytelling is an integral part of both the Jewish Passover and the Easter liturgy.

Large Group Activity: Easter Stories

Tell these stories yourself or **before the session** arrange with other members of the parish to be storytellers. Some storytellers may want to present their stories using hand puppets or a flannel board. Tips for telling a good story are included in the introduction of this book, pp. 9.

Story: Early in the Morning

Very early, one Sunday morning, two women walked to a tomb. Jesus had been killed on Friday. Jesus had been buried in the tomb on Friday. A large stone had been rolled in front of the tomb.

The women wept on Friday and on Saturday, too, as they remembered Jesus, so kind and good. Jesus had loved the women and had taught them—had even called them his own sisters. They wept for their brother, dead and buried.

On Sunday they walked to his tomb, but when they got there, the women stopped short—the stone was gone! The tomb looked dark and empty.

The women walked slowly to the door of the tomb. A young man, dressed in a white robe, sat there, but the body of Jesus was gone. The women were afraid. What could have happened? they wondered.

"Don't be afraid," the young man said. The women looked at him. "You are looking for Jesus," he said, "but Jesus is not here.

He is risen. He is alive. Go and tell all the friends of Jesus: you will see him again."

The women turned and ran from the tomb, filled with fear, filled with joy. They told their friends what the young man had said.

I wonder what the friends of Jesus thought when they heard the women's story so long ago. I wonder what you think when you hear their story today.

Story: The Road to Emmaus

Two friends of Jesus walked to a town called Emmaus one day. They felt sad—and puzzled. Jesus had died; they had seen him die and they knew he had been buried.

But now some of Jesus' friends were saying that he was alive again! The two friends who walked to Emmaus did not know what to think. A stranger saw them walking and began to walk with them.

"You seem sad," said the stranger.

"We are," the friends of Jesus answered. "Our friend Jesus was killed last Friday. But now some people say they have seen him alive. We miss him so much; we wish it were true, but how can a dead man live?"

"Well," said the stranger, "maybe it will help you if I tell you what scripture says about your friend Jesus." And the stranger began to tell stories to the friends, just as I am telling you a story now.

The friends felt happy as the stranger spoke. When they came to Emmaus, they did not want the stranger to leave. "Stay with us, sir," they said. "Please come and eat with us."

The stranger agreed and they came to where they would eat that night. The stranger picked up the bread, gave thanks to God, and broke the bread.

The friends gasped. They looked at the hands that broke the bread. They looked at the face of the stranger and saw no stranger, but Jesus himself, their dearest friend. Then he was gone.

The two friends got up at once, without eating, and ran back to the other friends of Jesus, waiting in Jerusalem. "We saw him," they shouted. "Jesus is truly alive!"

Story: Thomas Who Wanted to See for Himself

"I don't believe it. It just can't be true," Thomas said. He shook his head and turned to walk away.

"Wait, Thomas," his friend Matthew said. "It is true! We were all meeting in the room. And suddenly Jesus was right there with us!"

"How could it have been Jesus?" Thomas asked. "We saw him die and we saw his body put in the stone cave."

Growing Together

"Thomas, believe me. It was Jesus. It really was! He was as alive as you or me. We could even see the holes in his hands and feet where he was nailed to the cross," Matthew said.

"I wish I had been there," Thomas said.

Matthew put his hand on Thomas' shoulder. "Thomas, we will meet again next week. Maybe Jesus will be there again."

"Well," Thomas said slowly. "I'll be sure to be there next time, Matthew. But all I can say is, I want to see for myself. I want to touch the nail holes in Jesus' hands and feet. Otherwise, how can I believe Jesus is really alive again?"

All week long, Thomas thought about what his friend Matthew had said. Could Jesus be alive? Jesus had talked about becoming alive again. But Thomas himself had touched Jesus' cold dead body before it was shut away in the stone cave. Thomas knew he'd just have to see Jesus and touch him to believe that he was alive again.

When the day finally came for the meeting, Thomas could feel the excitement. Everyone was talking about the last time they had seen Jesus. Suddenly, everyone was very quiet. As Thomas turned around, he saw Jesus!

"Peace be with you," Jesus said to all of them. Then Jesus looked straight at Thomas. "Thomas," Jesus said gently. "Touch me—put your fingers in the nail holes. Believe that I am really alive." Jesus stretched out his hands for Thomas to touch.

Thomas couldn't stop looking at Jesus' face. It really was Jesus. Thomas had thought he would never see Jesus again. And here Jesus was, smiling at Thomas in the same loving way he had always smiled.

Thomas fell to his knees.

"My Lord and my God!" Thomas whispered. He knew he didn't have to touch Jesus' hands and feet to believe that Jesus was alive again.

Story: Breakfast with Jesus

Jesus had died. Jesus had risen. Jesus had appeared to his friends. A few days after Jesus appeared, the friends met again to discuss their plans. When would Jesus come again? What did Jesus want them to do?

Thomas watched Peter pace back and forth. "I'm tired of waiting with nothing to do," Peter exclaimed. "I'm going fishing."

Thomas wasn't surprised to hear Peter say that. After all, Peter had been a fisherman long before he had ever met Jesus. "Let's all go," Thomas said.

Early the next morning on the fishing boat, Thomas smiled at Peter. "It's good to be doing something," Thomas said.

"Well, it would be a lot better if we could catch some fish," Peter said glumly. "We've been fishing all night and haven't caught one yet."

Just then Thomas and Peter heard a shout from the shore. They saw a man standing on the beach waving at them. They waved back.

"Have you caught anything?" the man on the beach called.

"Not a thing!" Thomas and Peter shouted.

"Throw your net out on the other side of the boat," the man called back.

"What good would that do?" Thomas said to Peter.

"I don't know," Peter answered, "but we may as well give it a try."

They threw out the huge net on the other side of the boat. Almost at once fish started swimming into the net. Soon it was bulging; the fishermen could barely hold on.

Suddenly Peter yelled, "It's Jesus! It's the Lord." So Peter dove into the water and swam for shore.

When the other fishermen reached the shore, they found that Jesus had built a small fire. "Bring me some of the fish," Jesus said.

The friends of Jesus hurried to do as he asked. Jesus roasted the fish; then he broke bread and passed the food around. And Jesus, risen from the dead, sat down to eat breakfast with his friends.

Leader's Resources: Outreach

- Expand on the "Breakfast with Jesus" story and prepare an Easter breakfast for a homeless shelter or food distribution center, either on Easter Sunday or on a week-end later in the Easter season. Breakfast can often be bleak and uninspired at these places, and wonderful pastries, home-made coffee cakes and yummy breakfast breads can be a real treat. Invite families to prepare and deliver their delicious breakfast goodies in person.
- Take up an "Easter collection"—a great old Catholic tradition!—at the Easter session, to be distributed to the poor and needy. Ask families to decorate their own small donation envelopes and use them for the collection.

Growing Together

Large Group Activity:
Meditation (for older participants)

Materials

copies of questions (see **before the session**)

pens or pencils

Before the session prepare copies of these two questions, making one copy for each participant:

1. If I were one of the disciples in the upper room, I might have been feeling and thinking:
   a. I wish I had never gotten involved with these people.
   b. I feel that Jesus has let me down.
   c. I'm sad about what Jesus went through, but I'm glad it was Jesus and not me. I hope it doesn't happen to me.
   d. I really let Jesus down. He counted on me to support him. There must have been something more I could have done.
   e. Other:

2. If I had been there the night when Jesus appeared, I would have felt:
   a. surprised, confused
   b. joyful, elated
   c. shocked, afraid
   d. guilty, embarrassed
   e. other:

At the session pass out copies of the questions and pens or pencils. Ask the participants to imagine that they are gathered in a room on the night of the resurrection. Read aloud:

You are one of the disciples. You have traveled with Jesus for the past three years. You gave up everything to follow him. You were convinced that Jesus was the Messiah, but his death has put an end to all your hopes. You are no longer sure who he was; you wonder if your life is in danger, too.

This morning Mary Magdalene came to the room where you and other followers of Jesus are gathered. She said that she had seen Jesus alive. Peter and John had run to the tomb and found it empty. You are confused and upset. Why is Jesus' body missing? And what crazy hope are Mary, Peter, and John clinging to?

Now stop reading and ask each participant to answer the first question by circling or

underlining one choice. Allow two minutes. Invite participants to share their answers and the reasons for the answers. Then resume reading aloud:

Suddenly you see Jesus—in the locked room. How can this be? Is he real? Jesus holds out his hands; they have the marks of the nails by which he hung on the cross. Jesus speaks: "Peace be with you," he says. This is what Jesus always said.

Stop reading again and ask each participant to choose an answer to the second question. After two minutes, invite participants to share their answers and the reasons for those answers.

Closing Prayer

Choose one of these options:

● Choose one of the Easter stories from this session to proclaim from *The Lectionary for Masses with Children*.

● If you made Easter Prayer Books, end your session with a brief prayer service using these books.

● If you did the Easter Wheat Activity, you could sing "Now the Green Blade Riseth" as your closing prayer.

● Gather around the Easter tree, the cards or banner you made, or other visible fruits of your session. Pray: We thank you, Lord Jesus, for signs of new life: for butterflies, eggs, lilies, and lambs. Help us to see in these symbols the good news of Easter: that things which had grown old are being made new, that you are bringing all things to perfection. *Amen*.

● Pray: Dear God, we thank you for the miracle of Easter—for sending your Son, Jesus, to overcome death. When darkness or death separate us from you and from each other, give us faith to claim your life-giving Spirit. At the dawn of each day, let us awaken to a new Easter morning. *Amen*.

Pentecost

Introduction and Information

On the Day of Pentecost the Christian Church celebrates the gift of God's Holy Spirit given to God's holy people. Pentecost is also the Greek name for the Jewish Feast of Weeks, celebrated 50 days after Passover. On this feast, the first fruits of the wheat harvest were presented, and the covenant made with God at Mount Sinai was remembered and renewed.

In the Acts of the Apostles, Luke describes the promised outpouring of the Spirit and the beginning of the Church's mission as occurring in Jerusalem during this feast. The accounts in both Acts (Acts 2:1-4) and the Gospel of John (John. 20:22) depict the coming of the Holy Spirit to the disciples assembled together.

This assembly of the disciples emphasizes an important point: From the beginning, the experience of the Holy Spirit has been a corporate experience. Individuals as members of the Body of Christ participate in the experience, but the power of the Spirit is given for the life of the Church.

Two key words referring to the coming of the Holy Spirit are *promise* and *power*. The promise of Jesus to send the Helper to the disciples was fulfilled, and the power of that Helper was bestowed, in the upper room at Pentecost.

Signs of God's Power

Fire and wind are signs of the Spirit's power. Fire and wind signify God's power throughout the Old Testament. God goes before the people as a pillar of fire in the exodus; God sends a wind to part the Red Sea before them.

God's power is seen in the Pentecost story as the apostles proclaim Jesus Christ crucified and resurrected. The gift of tongues in Acts 2 is a sign that God's word is no longer limited to one people or one place, one language or one race, but is now available to all people everywhere.

The preaching of Peter on Pentecost responds to the question raised by his hearers: "What shall we do?" The apostle replies, "Each one of you must turn away from his sins and be baptized in the name of Jesus Christ, so that your sins will be forgiven; and you will receive God's gift, the Holy Spirit" (Acts 2:38).

This is still the Christian message—repentance, baptism, and the gift of the Holy Spirit. We, too, are called to preach the good news of Jesus Christ and to bring others to baptism.

Growing Together

Pentecost is sometimes referred to as "the birthday of the Church," but the birthday refers not to the institutional church, but rather to our birth into the new life of the risen Christ, the new creation that comes from the Holy Spirit. Pentecost brings the Easter season to an official end, but as with the neophytes in our parish, it also marks the beginning of our new life. Neophytes and long-time Christians alike can continue to reflect on the joys of Easter well past Pentecost. Through the gifts of the Holy Spirit, we are guided and supported in our attempts to live out our baptismal promises.

Symbolic Meanings

There are significant symbolic meanings in the Acts description of Pentecost. The Jewish feast commemorated the giving of the law on Mount Sinai. The gift of the Spirit to the Church on this feast fulfills the words of Jeremiah: "I will put my law within them, and I will write it on their hearts" (Jeremiah 31:33).

Pentecost also symbolizes the reversal of Babel in Genesis 11. At Babel, confusion, in the form of diverse languages, confounds the understanding of the builders. On Pentecost, the apostles are understood in every language. At Babel, the human city is scattered. On Pentecost, the city of God is drawn together as 3,000 believers are added to the Church.

The gift of tongues, given at Pentecost, is still part of the Church's experience of the power of the Holy Spirit today. But the power of the Spirit is manifested not only in such dramatic gifts as tongues and healing; scripture is clear that *any* positive response to God is the result of the work of the Holy Spirit. Paul emphasizes that we cannot even confess that Jesus is Lord unless we do so by the power of the Holy Spirit within us (1 Corinthians 12:3).

The Holy Spirit: God in Our Midst

The Holy Spirit is God dwelling in our midst, making real and effective the will of God for us and in us. In baptism the Holy Spirit incorporates us into Jesus Christ. In the Eucharist the Holy Spirit makes real the life-giving presence of Jesus Christ in the Bread and Wine.

The Holy Spirit inspires and guides the Church's teaching and preaching. The Holy Spirit moves God's people to works of mercy, mission, and evangelism.

The power given to the apostles and the early Church is given to us as well. We, too, are called to turn "the world upside down" (Acts 17:6). The promise is fulfilled; the power is given. Let God's people declare "God's deeds of power" (Acts 2:11).

Help! How do I plan this session?

How will I publicize this session?

_____

_____

How many people do I think might participate? _____

What are the ages of the participants?

_____

Where will we hold the session?

_____

Which recommended activities would work best with this particular group of participants? (Remember, we provide more activities than most groups can use in a single session. Pick a few that will work for your group.)

_____

_____

_____

_____

_____

_____

_____

Volunteers

to do	names	phone numbers
planning:		
preparation and set-up:		
activity leaders:		
clean-up:		

Growing Together

Session Plan

Gathering Prayer

Gathering Prayer

Sing "Veni, Creator Spiritus" or "We Are One in the Spirit, We Are One in the Lord."

Key Idea

Pentecost, Greek for *50 days*, was the Jewish feast celebrating the wheat harvest and the covenant made with God at Mount Sinai. The book of Acts associates the giving of the Holy Spirit with this feast.

Small Group Activity: Story Scramble

Materials

3" x 5" index cards
Bibles

Before the session write out Acts 2:1-4 on index cards, putting one word of the story on each card.

At the session pass out one or more cards to each participant. Ask the participants to

arrange the cards in the right order. (Bibles may be used to help find the correct order.)

When the participants have unscrambled the cards, ask one participant to read the cards aloud in their correct order.

Small Group Activity: Pentecost Newscast

Materials

Bibles

cardboard tubes from paper products to use as mock microphones

Have the participants prepare a newscast on the story of Pentecost. Ask one participant to serve as the news anchor person. This person will be in charge of introducing the story, asking each reporter to speak in turn, and concluding the story.

Divide the other participants into three groups as follows:

Group #1:
Presents the disciples' stories. Parts needed: reporter, Peter, other disciples.

Group #2:
Presents the bystanders' stories. Parts needed: reporter, bystanders from Parthia, Media, Elam, etc.

Group #3:

Presents the stories of the newly baptized. Parts needed: reporter, new believers.

Ask the participants to use Bibles to improvise interviews from Acts 2. Allow 15 minutes for work. Then have the participants present their Pentecost Newscast.

▶ Large Group Activity: Pentecost Story

Materials

wind instruments: flutes, pipes, half-filled pop bottles

red crepe paper streamers in 12" lengths, stapled together in bunches of 4-6

Divide the group into two choruses. Designate one chorus as *wind* and the other chorus as *fire*. Give *wind* the wind instruments. Give *fire* the paper streamers.

Invite the group to provide special effects for the following story. Each time you say the word *wind*, have the participants with wind instruments make wind noises. Each time you say the word *fire*, have the participants with streamers make waves of flame.

Read the following:

The friends of Jesus waited in Jerusalem for the gift that Jesus had promised before he had gone to God in heaven.

The friends talked about what Jesus had said and what Jesus had been like. They talked about their fears, too.

"I'm afraid I will forget some of the wonderful stories he told," said Mary Magdalene.

"I'm afraid I will be too scared to tell other people about who Jesus is," said James.

"I'm afraid I will never be able to go as far as he wanted," said Joanna. "He said to go to the whole world with the good news. But the whole world is a big place."

Peter nodded his head. "I don't feel able to do the job he gave us," he said. "The gift he promised is going to have to be a powerful gift indeed if we are ever going to be able to find the memories and courage and strength to carry on."

The friends fell silent. A noise began to grow and grow, rushing to fill the house. "What is it?" asked Mary Magdalene. "It sounds like the mightiest of *winds*."

"Maybe it's the surprise Jesus promised," Joanna whispered. "I feel excitement in my heart."

"Me too!" exclaimed Peter. "My heart feels on *fire*."

Growing Together

The friends looked at each other with wide eyes. They were amazed to see *fire*, glowing over the head of each friend. They were amazed to hear the *wind* roar through the room.

Soon neighbors gathered from all around, outside the house. "What is the commotion?" they asked, some laughing, some cross. "What is all this noise at nine o'-clock in the morning?"

Jesus' friends felt the *wind* against their faces and saw the *fire* dance about. Then they ran outside to tell each neighbor—and then all the world—about Jesus, whose stories and courage and strength filled their hearts.

Leader's Tip

Emphasize the fact that Pentecost comes at the close of the Easter season, and that it is appropriate to add these final Easter celebrations:

● Add Pentecost symbols—such as doves and tongues of fire—to the Easter Tree (p. 56).

● Sing Easter hymns for the last time this year.

● If your parish celebrates Easter with food—such as a buffet of Easter treats—hold the same meal on Pentecost. Invite strangers or neighbors to join the feast.

Key Idea

The feast of Pentecost celebrates the gift of the Holy Spirit, promised by Jesus to his Church.

Large Group Activity: Scripture Meditation

Note: This meditation has a strong sensual element, making it suitable for mixed age groups. Do not expect younger participants to meditate in an adult fashion, but support their involvement in the story with a lively—but measured—reading, and with a personal example of quiet reflection.

Ask the participants to sit in a comfortable position as you read this scripture meditation:

"O Lord, the fire of your love has inflamed our hearts!" The followers of Jesus continue to sing their praise over and over again as they spontaneously form a circle and begin to dance.

Hands, joined together, swing back and forth as they form a joyful unit of praise... "We have felt the mighty force of your power, O Yahweh!" John half sings, half shouts, his face and eyes radiant with joy.

The circle widens as others join in, skipping and laughing and at the same time keeping the beat of an ancient tribal song of Israel. "Praise God for he has shown forth his glory!"

Andrew sings as Matthew loudly stamps his feet in rhythm to the singing. No one seems surprised as their chanting comes out in strange syllables. This has been happening to each of them since the strange wind and tongues of fire filled the room.

Mary of Magdala breaks into the center of the circle and with a lighthearted laugh begins to twist and turn in a dance of rapture. Hands clap in rhythm and voices sing songs of praise and joy to God. "Our hearts are full, O Lord," Simon sings.

James continues Simon's praise, "The breath of your Spirit is indeed upon us, O Lord." The tempo of the dance accelerates.

The effervescent feeling and the overwhelming peace within you are unexplainable. You, too, become more and more involved in this dance of exaltation, allowing all the joy within you to burst forth in dance.

Some of you now leave the circle and sit down to catch your breath. This gives you time to recall your experience. When it first happened, it was like a wave coming over you: first the great joy that almost burst your heart and then the peace flowing through you, calming you, and banishing all your fears. You felt then—and feel now—that you could go out and conquer the world for Jesus.

Peter joins you, breathless and perspiring. "I knew Jesus would come again and would not leave us alone," he tells you. His voice is so filled with love that his words become a prayer. "He promised to send his Spirit, and see how his promise is fulfilled!" Peter's hand sweeps the room as he speaks. "It's beyond our wildest dreams!"

Peter looks into your eyes, as his hands press firmly against his knees, and says, "How could I have doubted and been filled with such fear? As long as I was with the Lord, he never went back on his word." Peter smiles, shakes his head, stands, and looks down at you. "He is here now; he is with us. Do you feel his presence?" Peter leaves to rejoin the circle of dance.

Pause for a moment, then ask the participants to close their eyes and reflect on the following questions:
- Are you aware of the Lord's presence in your life?
- Does any doubt within you make you hesitate to go forth in his name?

After 4-5 minutes, conclude by leading the participants in praying the Lord's Prayer.

Growing Together

Small Group Activity: Gift Lists

Materials

Bible
28" x 40" poster board
felt pens
paper
pens or pencils

Before the session prepare a poster labeled: Thank God for the gifts given to *(the name of your parish)*.

At the session ask participants to use felt pens to draw pictures of wrapped gifts around the borders of the poster. Invite each participant to write a list of gifts or talents he or she possesses. Ask older participants to write for younger participants, helping younger participants with these or similar questions:

- What do you like to do most of all?
- What do you know how to do?
- What does your family like to see you do?

Divide the participants into groups of three or four. *Directions to the participants:*

- Ask someone in your group to pick three items on his or her list to read aloud.
- Then ask other members of your group to suggest two or more gifts that belong on the person's list.
- Repeat this process until each member of your group has read the list and received new gifts.

Reconvene the group. Ask each participant to pick three gifts from his or her list to write on the poster. Then gather the group around the poster to read 1 Corinthians 12:4-11 and to pray.

Invite each participant to take a turn completing this prayer:

Thank you, God, for *(name your parish)*'s gift of *(name one item from the poster)*.

When each participant has prayed, finish by praying:

- We give you thanks, God, for what you have given to each of us and all of us. Help each of us use our gifts to strengthen the work of *(name your parish)*; through Jesus Christ our Lord. *Amen*.

Leader's Tip

Ask participants before the session to bring in other wind toys such as:
- ready-made kites
- pinwheels
- wind chimes

After each wind activity, chant together this prayer:

> Come, wind of the Spirit, come.
> Fill us with your power and love.
> Come, wind of the Spirit, come.

Leader's Resources: Outreach

- Invite someone from the diocesan Mission Office or from the Jesuit Volunteer Corps to come to the Pentecost session to describe and discuss their programs. Missionary work is a vibrant and important ministry within Catholicism, and children of all ages are usually inspired by the stories of missionaries.

- A few weeks **before the session** contact the National Catholic Office with Disabilities (P.O. Box 29113, Washington, D.C. 20017) for handouts and materials that are useful in discussing ways for your parish to be more welcoming, inclusive and accommodating to person with special needs. Discuss this issue with participants during this Pentecost session, naming the many gifts that persons with disabilities bring to our church.

▶ Large Group Activity: Bible Study (for older participants)

Materials

Bibles
chalkboard and chalk or newsprint and marker

Invite participants to study the gift of the Holy Spirit in the promises of Jesus and the story of Pentecost. Distribute Bibles to the participants.

Ask participants to look up each Bible passage as you read the reference. Ask the participants to search each passage for attributes of the Holy Spirit. Write all the attributes mentioned on chalkboard or newsprint.

References:

Luke 12:12	John 14:16-17
John 3:8	John 14:26
John 4:23-24	John 15:26-27
John 6:63	John 16:7-8
John 7:37-39	John 16:13-15

Then ask participants to turn to Acts 2 in their Bibles. Ask one participant to read Acts 2:1-17 aloud. Discuss:

- What attributes from the list we made does this story suggest?
- What other attributes of the Holy Spirit does this story suggest?
- How would you describe the power of the Holy Spirit in these Bible passages?

Divide the participants into small groups of four or five to discuss:

- What evidence can you give that the Church is empowered by the Holy Spirit today?
- What challenges does our parish face that require us to rely on the power of the Holy Spirit?

Growing Together

Key Idea

The Gospel of John places the story of the giving of the Holy Spirit in the context of a new creation: the Church, filled with the Spirit, blessed with God's peace, and sent to offer God's forgiveness to the world.

Large Group Activity: Church Birthday Party

Invite participants to celebrate the birthday of the Church, using whatever materials are readily available. Suggestions follow:

Decorations
- crepe paper streamers
- construction paper chains in red, orange, and yellow
- inflated balloons decorated with doves drawn with felt markers

Refreshments
- Red foods, such as strawberries, cranberry juice, or bread spread with raspberry jam

- *Pentecost cake:* Make or purchase a sheet cake with chocolate frosting. Cut a piece of waxed paper the size of the surface of the cake. Cut out dove shapes from the waxed paper; then place the paper over the surface of the cake. Sift powdered sugar over the cake.
- *Gumdrop balloons:* Insert pretzel sticks into large gumdrops. Use the gumdrop balloons to decorate cupcakes, or collect bunches of gumdrop balloons in small paper cups.

Activities
- Choose activities from the crafts, stories, or games in this chapter.

Small Group Activity: Pictures of Peace

Materials

> Bible
> paper
> pens or pencils
> crayons or felt pens

Read John 20:19-23 aloud to the participants. Ask participants to divide into pairs. Encourage older participants to pair with younger ones.

Ask the pairs to begin by talking about peace: What does peace mean to each participant? Then invite each pair of participants to produce a picture and poem about peace. Each pair may divide the work in whatever way is most comfortable.

Each poem should begin with these words: *Peace comes when...* Ask participants writing poems to limit their poems to no more than eight lines.

Allow 15 minutes for work; then reconvene the group. Invite pairs to show their pictures and to read their poems. If possible, arrange the finished work in a display on a wall of your building.

Leader's Resources: Multicultural Issues

- Read *Africa Dream*, a short story book by Eloise Greenfield, to discover the richness of God's gifts of memory and imagination. Prepare to discuss ways in which the lives of our ancestors can affect who we are today.

- Invite participants to compose prayer intentions for the needs of the Church, the parish community, the poor, the sick and those who have died. Read the "prayers of petition" and sing the response, "Oyenos, Mi Dios," by Bob Hurd. Include other languages as well: "Listen to your people" (English), "Dinggin Mo Kami" (Tagalog) and "Xin Lang Nghe Loi Con" (Vietnamese).

- Other suitable songs for Pentecost include the traditional "In Christ There Is No East or West," based on the text from Galatians 3:28. This passage might be proclaimed and discussed prior to singing the song. The Holy Spirit "weaves one heart from the many strands" of culture present in our Church. Sing "Weave One Heart" by Marty Haugen, (GIA Publications, Inc., 1993) and practice the Hawaiian refrain.

Growing Together

Key Idea

Fire is a sign of God's power, associated with the coming of the Holy Spirit at Pentecost.

Large Group Activity: Candle Light Story

Materials

Bible(s)
candles
matches

Before the session ask for volunteers from your parish who can speak languages other than English. Ask them to prepare to read Acts 2:1-4 in those other languages.

At the session gather participants in a circle. Darken the room and light one candle. Read Acts 2:1-4 to the participants. Then have each volunteer take a turn lighting a candle and reading Acts 2:1-4 in his or her chosen language.

Small Group Activity: Fire Messages

Materials

tissue paper in red, orange, yellow, and gold
9" x 12" construction paper
large stapler
crayons or felt pens

Have participants cut flame shapes from the tissue paper. Have each participant arrange a group of shapes on construction paper. The base of the flames should be 1 inch away from the bottom of a 9" edge on the construction paper. Have each participant group the flame shapes so that a single staple will attach the flames at their bases to the construction paper. Have the participants leave the tops of the flames loose.

Invite each participant to write a Pentecost message on the paper, completing the sentence:

Pentecost is...

_____ *(Fill in a sound.)*

_____ *(Fill in a sight.)*

_____ *(Fill in a feeling.)*

_____ *(Fill in a thought about the meaning of Pentecost.)*

Read each other's completed messages and take them home to think about.

Small Group Activity: Fire Crafts

Choose one or more of these Fire Crafts for the session.

Acetate Flames

Materials

acetate in red, yellow, and orange
scissors
rubber cement
Optional:
thread
black markers

Note: Transparent report covers, available at office supply stores, provide an inexpensive source of acetate.

Directions to the participants: Cut flame shapes from the acetate. Use rubber cement to glue together the flames in fan shapes. You may want to attach thread so that the shapes can be hung on an Easter Tree or in windows. You may also write one word on each shape to spell: *The Spirit of God is here.*

Paper Candles

Materials

cardboard tubes from paper products
construction paper
scissors
glue
tissue paper in red, orange, and yellow
felt marker

Directions to the participants: Take a tube and cut construction paper to fit around the tube. Write on the paper: *The flame of the Spirit.* Glue the construction paper around the tube. Cut flame shapes from the tissue paper and paste them to the inside of the cardboard tube.

Growing Together

Flame Hats

Materials

tissue paper in red, orange, and yellow
scissors
stapler
12" x 18" white paper
colored markers

Directions to the participants: To make
flames, cut sheets of tissue paper into 8" x
15" rectangles. Layer together three rectangles of tissue paper in different colors.

Roll the layered rectangles into a 15" tube.
Make four evenly-spaced cuts, each cut
3 inches long, at one end of the tube.
Moisten a finger and insert it into the cut
end of the tube. Carefully pull the inner
rolls out while gently holding the top with
the other hand. Staple the center and end
of the tube.

Make a hat by taking a 12" x 18" sheet
of paper. Cut a 12" circle from the paper.
Make a 6-inch cut from the outside of the
circle to the center. With a marker, write

Happy Day of Pentecost on the hat. Form
a hat by overlapping the cut edges of the
paper. Staple the hat to hold its shape.
Staple the flames to the hat.

▶ Small Group Activity:
Game (for younger participants)

Materials

Flame Hats (see activity above)

This game is a variation of "Duck, Duck,
Goose." Invite the participants to sit in a
circle. Designate one player as *it*. Give *it*
a Flame Hat.

Holding the hat, *it* circles the seated players, touching each participant on the head
and saying: "The Holy Spirit, the Holy
Spirit, etc." until *it* chooses one player by
saying "the Holy Spirit is *here*," and drops
the Flame Hat on that player's head.

The player who receives the Flame Hat
must chase *it* around the circle as *it* tries
to run to the chosen player's place. If
it reaches the place before he or she is
caught, then the chosen player becomes
the new *it*. If *it* is caught, *it* must take the
hat back and try again.

Any successful *it* should be given a Flame
Hat to wear once seated. New *its* can only
choose players who do not yet wear
Flame Hats.

Key Idea

Wind is a sign of God's power, associated with the coming of the Holy Spirit at Pentecost.

Small Group Activity: Bible Study (for older participants)

Materials

Bibles

copies of the Wind Study Sheet, found at the end of this activity

Ask the participants to divide into five small groups to study the concept of *wind* in the Bible. Ask one participant in each group to serve as leader and give him or her a copy of the Wind Study Sheet.

Assign each group *one* of these readings:
● Genesis 8:1-19
● Exodus 14:10-29
● Numbers 11:4-6, 31-32
● Ezekiel 37:1-10
● John 3:1-8

Allow 15 minutes for the groups to work. Then reconvene the group and read Acts 2. Lead a discussion on this passage using the questions on the Wind Study Sheet.

Wind Study Sheet

1. What words could we use to describe wind in this story?

2. What is accomplished through wind in this story?

3. How is wind a sign of God's power in this story?

4. What promises of God are fulfilled in this story?

Large Group Activity: Balloon Messages

Materials

scissors
paper
pens or pencils
red balloons
tank of helium
Optional:
chalkboard and chalk or newsprint
   and marker

Ask each participant to write a Pentecost message on a strip of paper. Ask older participants to help younger ones.

You may wish to generate a list of possible Pentecost messages by beginning with a brainstorming session in which you ask these or similar questions:
● Why does God send us the Holy Spirit?
● How is the Holy Spirit like wind and fire?
● What does the Holy Spirit empower us to do?
● What message does God want us to give to the world?

Growing Together

● What do you know about God's Spirit that gives meaning to your life?

Write all suggestions on chalkboard or newsprint. When each participant has a message ready, give him or her a red balloon in which the message may be inserted. Have someone prepared to fill each balloon with helium and to tie the opening with a string.

Invite participants to take balloon messages home for friends, family members and neighbors.

Large Group Activity: Wind Play

Invite participants to enjoy playing with the wind today.

Sack Kites

Materials

  lunch sacks or heavyweight white
    plastic trash bags
  felt markers or crayons
  glue or stapler
  strips of red, yellow, and orange crepe
    paper
  hole punch
  6' lengths of string or yarn, 1 per sack

Directions to the participants: Take a sack or bag and decorate it with felt markers or crayons. Use glue or staples to attach a tail of crepe paper streamers to the sack at one corner.

Punch a hole in the other end of the sack. Tie a 6-foot length of string or yarn to the sack. Take your Sack Kite outside to fly.

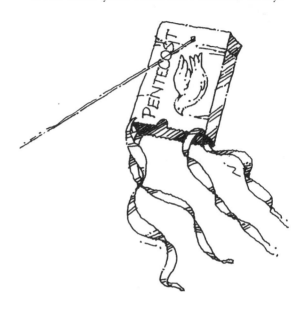

Parachutes

Materials

  either a parachute or a circle of light-
    weight fabric
  handkerchiefs or bandannas
  string
  scissors
  small wooden blocks

Invite a group of participants to take a parachute outside and lift it overhead, bringing it down with the trapped air resisting the participants' movements. Have the participants ripple the parachute up and down.

If you can't find a parachute, try an old lightweight sheet or curtain, trimmed into a circle or oval shape. This "parachute" may tear if the edge isn't hemmed.

Individual parachutes may be made from handkerchiefs or bandannas, string, and blocks of wood. ***Directions to the participants:***

- Take a handkerchief or bandanna. Tie one string to each corner.
- Tie the four ends of the strings around a small wooden block. Gently loft the parachute into the air.

 ## Closing Prayer

- Gather participants in a circle, placing a lighted candle in the center of the circle. Ask participants to focus on the flame and to imagine that each one of them is filled with the warmth and light of that flame. Ask them to think about the effects of their flame coming in contact with the flames of the others in the room. Then spend time thanking God for the power and light that the Holy Spirit will spread into the world through this group.

- If the group took part in the Gift Lists activity (p. 80), invite participants to review their personal lists and to volunteer prayers of thanksgiving for opportunities to serve God with their gifts. Then collect the lists in a basket, committing these gifts to God by placing the basket on the altar during congregational worship.

- Have participants form a circle, asking the youngest children to hold hands and to stand in a circle within the larger group. Ask the older participants to place their hands on the heads or shoulders of the children. Have a time of spontaneous prayer, especially inviting the children to give thanks for something God has given them. Then invite older participants to pray for the younger, committing the lives and gifts of the children to God.

Summer Celebration of God's Creation

Introduction and Information

"The world is charged with the grandeur of God," wrote Gerard Manley Hopkins, and Trinity Sunday—or any day in summer—is an excellent day to delight in that grandeur. Christians may be called a "people of the book," but they are also a people called to rejoice in God's good creation.

This joy is part of our Jewish heritage. Many people are aware that the creation stories of Genesis are paralleled in the creation myths of other Mesopotamian peoples; fewer people are aware of what sets the biblical stories apart.

In Genesis, creation is no accident of an absent-minded god, but the loving intention of the One God. Nor are men and women created to be the slaves of the gods, but to be the crown of God's creation. Men and women are made to delight in the creation that delights its Creator.

This heritage of joy in the creation can also be seen in many of the psalms, such as Psalm 104, which praises God who makes "springs gush forth in the valleys," where wild donkeys "quench their thirst" (Psalm 104:10). Psalm 148 and Psalm 150 call upon the whole creation to respond to its Creator in praise: "Let everything that breathes praise the Lord!" (Psalm 150:6)

This loving response to the Creator is the special vocation of humanity, made in God's image. Dorothy L. Sayers, in *The Mind of the Maker*, shows that creative work itself is the response of love appropriate to humanity.

Sayers points out that the story in which humanity is described as being made in God's image is a story in which God is shown doing only one thing: creating. Since God is Trinity, our own work as creators can be understood as a trinitarian activity. In other words, an understanding of the Trinity can illumine our understanding of creative work—and an understanding of our creativity can illumine our understanding of the Trinity.

Issues of creativity lie at the very heart of Christian formation, because to live a life of grace is to live creatively. Christians are not called merely to submit to a set of divine rules, still less to conform to the structures of an unjust society, but to remake the world into God's kingdom.

To help people become aware of themselves as creators, called to collaborate with the creative God, is a fundamental quest of Christian education. For children, this may be accomplished by inviting them

Growing Together

to experience their powers as creators in a variety of media. For adults, these experiences may take second place to reflections upon experiences already gained.

But both adults and children will need to experience or recall the qualities of creative work found in a child's play. Watch a child at play, perhaps building a tower of wooden blocks. His or her work is often distinguished by persistence, attentiveness, and painstaking care. This absorption in the work at hand rather than in the self is the quality that must characterize us as Christian workers and creators.

This summer, let us recover our sense of delight in God's creation. As we rejoice in this world of trees and sand, sidewalks and manhole covers, let us rededicate ourselves to the work and play for which we were born. Let us remember our inheritance as creatures made in the image of God, who "saw everything that he had made, and indeed, it was very good" (Genesis 1:31).

Help! How do I plan this session?

How will I publicize this session?

_____
_____

How many people do I think might participate? _____

What are the ages of the participants?

_____

Where will we hold the session?

_____

Which recommended activities would work best with this particular group of participants? (Remember, we provide more activities than most groups can use in a single session. Pick a few that will work for your group.)

_____
_____
_____
_____
_____
_____
_____

Volunteers

to do	names	phone numbers
planning:		
preparation and set-up:		
activity leaders:		
clean-up:		

Growing Together

Session

Gathering Prayer

Pray together Psalm 8 or sing together Came Down/Siyahamba (We Are Marching) from the Iona Community, available through GIA Publications.

Key Idea

The creation stories of the Bible portray creation as the purposeful act of a loving God.

Small Group Activity: Creation Story

Materials

Optional:
children's Bible

Read the story of creation to the participants, using a children's Bible, if possible. If not, read Genesis 1:1–2:3.

Then divide the participants into seven groups. Invite each group to prepare either a tableau or a pantomime to illustrate one day in the creation story. Then read the story again, asking each group to form its tableau or pantomime at your signal.

Note: A tableau is a composition of people in a single, fixed position, comparable to a snapshot. A pantomime involves silent motion. Allow the group members to choose the medium of presentation that seems most appropriate for the events of their assigned "day."

Small Group Activity: Creative Pursuit Game

Materials

sheets of newsprint or scrap paper
felt markers
Bibles
cake or other refreshment

Invite participants to play a game of Creative Pursuit to test their knowledge of God's creation and of the Genesis story.

Give each participant four sheets of newsprint or scrap paper. Ask each participant to number his or her sheets of paper from *one* to *four*.

Divide the participants into groups of six or seven. Designate one participant in each group as *leader*. Give a Bible to each leader.

Ask each leader to stand in a fixed position. Ask the other participants of each group to form a circle around their group's leader.

Ask each participant to use his or her sheets of paper to make a straight path to the leader. Each path should begin with a paper numbered *one*, and end, next to the leader, with a paper numbered *four*. Ask each participant to stand on *one*.

Directions to the leaders: Beginning with one participant and moving in a clockwise direction, ask each participant in your group a question about the creation story in Genesis 1:1–2:4 or a general question about God's creation.

Tailor your questions to each participant. Difficult questions might include:

- What did God create on the fifth day? *(Genesis 1:20-23)*
- What food did God provide for the wild animals and birds? *(Genesis 1:30)*
- What is the first verse of the creation story? *(Genesis 1:1)*

Simple questions might include:

- What animal in God's creation says "meow"?
- Can you name a food from God's creation that is sweet?
- Can you name a flower in God's creation that is red?

If a participant answers correctly, invite that participant to step to the next paper on the path.

Directions to the groups: When each participant in your group is on a paper numbered *four*, give this signal *(name a signal)*. The first group to signal wins the prize. **Note:** Choose a signal **before the session**.

Provide a cake or other refreshment for everyone. Ask the winning team to serve the cake to the other participants.

▶ Small Group Activity:
Bible Study (for older participants)
Materials

Bibles
paper
pens or pencils

Distribute Bibles to the participants. Ask one participant to read aloud Genesis 1:1–2:3. Discuss:

- How would you describe God the Creator in this story? *(Consider asking each participant to give a one-word answer.)*
- How are man and woman different from the other creatures of God?
- How are man and woman similar to the other creatures of God?
- In what sense are we made like God or made in God's image?
- How would you describe God's Word in this story?

Ask another participant to read aloud John 1:1-5. Discuss:

- How would you describe God's word in this passage?
- How does this story illumine the story of Genesis 1:1–2:4?
- How does Genesis 1:1—2:4 illumine the story of John 1:1-5?

Divide the participants into small groups of four to five participants. Invite each small group to write its own story of creation that includes the insights of both Genesis 1:1–2:4 and John 1:1-5.

Growing Together

Leader's Resources: Outreach

- View the 10-minute video "The Mouse's Tale" from Catholic Relief Services (209 West Fayette Street, Baltimore MD 21201), an animated story addressing causes of world hunger and issues of social justice. Allow time for discussion.
- Read and discuss the children's book *The Wall*, by Eve Bunting (New York: Clarion Books, 1990), a story of the Vietnam Veterans Memorial and an illustration of the goodness of God's creative life that continues beyond death.

Key Idea

The Jewish heritage of joy in the creation can be seen in many of the psalms of praise.

Small Group Activity: Mural

Materials

    Bibles
    masking tape
    roll of butcher paper or newsprint
    scissors
    construction paper in assorted colors
    glue
    crayons
    felt pens

Invite participants to make a mural illustrating Psalm 104. Divide participants into nine mixed-age groups. Distribute Bibles and assign each group a set of verses from Psalm 104:

- *Group one:* verses 1-4
- *Group two:* verses 5-9
- *Group three:* verses 10-12
- *Group four:* verses 13-15
- *Group five:* verses 16-18
- *Group six:* verses 19-23
- *Group seven:* verses 24-26
- *Group eight:* verses 27-30
- *Group nine:* verses 31-34

Tape a long sheet of butcher paper or newsprint to a table or the floor, allowing one or two feet of paper for each participant. (If necessary, have each group make a separate mural.)

Invite each group of participants to illustrate its set of verses using bits of construction paper and drawings with crayons and felt pens. Hang the finished mural(s) in a public part of the building.

Small Group Activity: Psalm Writing (for older participants)

Materials

Bible
chalkboard and chalk or newsprint
    and marker
paper
pens or pencils

Read aloud Psalm 148 to the participants. Ask the participants to list all the parts of creation and society the psalmist calls upon to praise the Lord. Record all answers on chalkboard or newsprint.

Discuss:
- What other parts of creation and contemporary society could be invited to praise the Lord? Record all suggestions on chalkboard or newsprint.

Ask participants to work together to write their own versions of Psalm 148. Divide participants into small groups of five or six.

Invite each group to write 10 verses that invite creation and society to praise the Lord. Ask each group of participants to begin and end its psalm with "Hallelujah!" or "Praise the Lord!"

Allow 15 minutes for work. Then reconvene the entire group and ask each small group to read its psalm aloud to the other participants.

Large Group Activity: Praising God with Sound

Materials

Bible

Read Psalm 150 aloud to the group. Explain that when this psalm was read aloud in the temple a pause after each verse was filled with the sounds named.

Ask participants to improvise a psalm of praise to God with sound. Begin by asking participants to think of loud noises that could praise the Lord: the roar of tigers, the clapping of hands, or the crash of lightning.

Then ask one participant to complete this sentence: Praise the Lord with *(name a loud noise)*. Invite the other participants to imitate that noise as well as possible. Encourage a loud—even rowdy—game of praise to the Lord.

Ask another participant to complete the sentence above. Continue for 15 minutes or for as long as interest is sustained. Then conclude by reading the last verse of Psalm 150.

Growing Together

Key Idea

Our understanding of the Trinity can illumine our understanding of creative work, and our understanding of creative work can illumine our understanding of the Trinity.

Small Group Activity: Drawings and Discussion

Materials

12" x 18" paper
felt pens or crayons

Directions to the participants: Draw one picture from this list:

- a picture of your family
- a picture of your parish family
- a picture of you and your colleagues at work
- a picture of you and your classmates at school

Allow 10-15 minutes for work; then divide the participants into small groups of three to four participants. Ask the participants in each group to show their pictures and to discuss the following:

- What are some ways all the people in your picture are alike?
- What makes each person in your picture unique? *(You might reword this question for younger participants as:*

Can you tell us one special thing about each person in your picture?)

Allow 10 minutes for discussion; then reconvene the large group to discuss:

- In what ways do you think God is like the people in our pictures?
- In what ways do you think God is different from the people in our pictures?

Leader's Tip

  Satisfaction in work is absent from the employment experience of most adults. Some polls say that 80% of employed adults are dissatisfied with their jobs. Perhaps no issues of Christian education are more relevant to adult daily life than the issues of vocation and livelihood.

What Color is Your Parachute?, by Richard Bolles (Berkeley: Ten Speed, updated annually), is the classic career guide predicated on the religious conviction that humans were created to do the work they love best. This book makes an excellent resource for adult study groups.

 Other popular career resources are:
- *Do What You Love and the Money Will Follow* by Marsha Sinetar (New York: Dell, 1989)
- *Wishcraft: How to Get What You Really Want* by Barbara Sher (New York: Ballantine, 1979)
- *Do What You Are* by Paul D. Tieger and Barbara Barron-Tieger (Boston: Little, Brown and Company, 1992)

Leader's Resources: Multicultural Issues

- Sing "How Great Thou Art" using the Hawaiian translation "Ke Akua Mana E" from Manna Music, Inc., 1981.

- Beginning with the feast of Corpus Christi, summer offers many Sunday readings that focus on bread, loaves and fishes and Eucharist. Invite participants to taste (or prepare!) breads from many cultures: Mexican tortillas, pita breads from the Middle East, Bibingka cake from the Philippines, etc. View the classic video "Grandma's Bread" (St. Anthony Messenger Press) and make the connection between remembering and Eucharist.

▶ Small Group Activity: Discussion (for older participants)

Materials

    newsprint
    felt markers
    paper
    pens or pencils

Write the word *creator* in large, bold letters in the center of a large sheet of newsprint. Ask the participants to brainstorm synonyms for the word *creator*. Invite participants to record their ideas (words, phrases, or even simple sketches) on the newsprint. Allow time for participants to enjoy one another's ideas and to discuss anything that needs some explanation.

For the discussion activity, you may need to refresh your participants' understanding of the rules of brainstorming:

- Accept all ideas. This is not the time for analysis or criticism.
- Encourage participants to work quickly. This is not the time for lengthy reflections.
- Encourage participants to consider a variety of angles to the question and offer all possibilities to the group.

Distribute paper and pens or pencils. Now invite each participant to brainstorm a list of ways in which he or she is a *creator*. Allow three or four minutes for this work; then ask each participant to circle one favorite activity as a creator from his or her list.

Growing Together

Discuss:

- How would you describe God the Father's role in creation?
- In what way do humans display these characteristics as creators?
- How would you describe God the Son's role in creation?
- In what way do humans display these characteristics as creators?
- How would you describe the Holy Spirit's role in creation?
- In what way do humans display these characteristics as creators?

Divide the participants into small groups of four to five participants each. Ask each participant to name his or her favorite activity as a creator. Invite the participants in each small group to discuss:

- How do these activities display the creative characteristics of the Trinity?
- How do these activities reveal us as made in God's image?

Key Idea

Christians are a people called to rejoice in God's good creation.

Guide to Outdoor Activities

The general format suggested for these activities is a collection walk—a walk during which participants collect sights, sounds, or specific items. You may prefer to plan the entire session for an outdoor location.

Activities for exploring three common items in our environment—trees, sand, and weeds—are included below. Here are tips and activities useful for *any* environmental exploration:

- Give thought to a suitable location for your activities. Perhaps you have a beach or park available to you, or perhaps only an empty lot in the middle of the city. Help your participants celebrate the goodness of God's creation whatever your location.
- **Before the session** plan which activities will be done while walking, which activities will be done at the chosen location, and which activities will be done at the parish before or after the walk.
- Do not distinguish between "natural" items, such as flowers and trees, and "manmade" items, such as manhole covers and fire hydrants. *All* creation is sustained by God—and most flowers and trees today have been planned, planted, and sustained by people.
- If you are exploring an urban environment, do not, for this session, focus on litter or signs of decay. Look for grass growing in the cracks of sidewalks, pigeons cooing on the ledges of abandoned buildings, and old bricks laid in intricate patterns.

- Useful materials on any walk include binoculars, hand lenses, magnifying glasses, and collection containers, such as backpacks, envelopes, tote bags, or plastic grocery sacks.

Nature Collage

Materials

newsprint or butcher paper
glue

Ask participants to make a collage of items found on the collection walk.

Collection Comparison

Materials

paper
pens or pencils

If your location is your parish's own yard or neighborhood, divide the participants into small groups. Ask each group's members to make a list of what they think they will find on the collection walk. Then ask group members to list what they actually find on the walk. Have the groups compare lists *after* the walk.

Creation Fables

Materials

manila envelopes

Divide participants into small groups. Ask each group to pick out three items from its walk and put them into a manila envelope. Have the groups exchange envelopes. Then have each group make up a tall tale about the items in its envelope.

Praise Mural

Materials

newsprint or butcher paper
glue or tape
crayons or felt markers

After the walk, ask the participants to make a mural called "Praise God from A to Z." Invite the participants to decorate the murals with an alphabetical arrangement of items found on the walk, such as acorns, bird feathers, cattails, etc. Have the participants fill in any missing letters with drawings. Invite children to decorate the border of your mural.

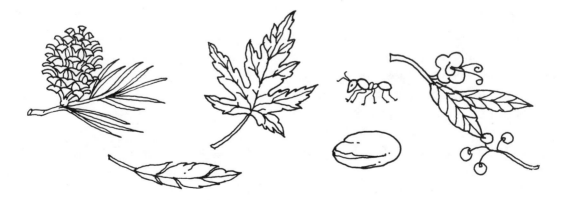

Growing Together

Creation Rubbings

Materials

paper
crayons

Provide paper and peeled crayons to make rubbings on the collection walks. Consider such subjects as tree bark, manhole covers, rocks, leaves, etc. Place a piece of paper over the object and rub the paper lightly with the side of a crayon.

Sun Pictures

Materials

blueprint paper
box
tape
hydrogen peroxide

After the walk, invite the participants to make sun pictures of items found on the walk. **Before the session** obtain blueprint paper at a camera store.

In a darkened room, have the participants tape items with distinctive shapes—leaves, grasses, feathers, etc.—to the blueprint paper.

Then have the participants put the prepared paper into a closed box, carry the box outside, and expose the paper to sunlight for a few minutes. Close the box and bring it inside before removing the taped items. (To prevent the pictures from fading, dip each paper into a solution of 1/4 cup of 3% hydrogen peroxide dissolved in 2 cups of water.)

Bible Search

Materials

Bible concordance

Ask older participants to find passages in the Bible that name the items being explored, such as trees, sand, and weeds or grass. Ask these participants to read the passages aloud as the other participants work. (A Bible Concordance would simplify the search for the items named.)

Small Group Activity: Exploring Trees

Invite participants to explore trees with one or more of the following activities.

Discover a Tree

Directions to the participants:

- Put your arms around the tree. How far do your arms reach?
- Smell the tree in different places: at the roots, on the bark, and at a leaf.
- What lives in the tree? Check the branches, the bark, and the roots.
- Can you make the shape of this tree with your body? How is this tree shaped differently from another tree?

Bird Feeders

Materials

plastic knife
pine cones
peanut butter
bird seeds
string or yarn
suet
plastic mesh onion bags
popcorn
needles
thread
Optional:
crumbs
raisins
cranberries

Invite the participants to make Bird Feeders to hang in the tree(s). **Directions to the participants:**

- Use a plastic knife to smear a pine cone with peanut butter. Roll the cone in bird seeds. Tie string or yarn to the cone and hang on a branch.
- Melt suet over low heat. Stir in bird seeds until cool. You may add peanut butter and crumbs if you wish. Form the mixture into balls. Put one ball into each plastic mesh bag. Tie string or yarn to the bag and hang on a branch.
- Pop the popcorn. Use a needle to string the popcorn onto a thread. You may add raisins or cranberries to the thread if they are available. Hang on a branch.

Directions to the participants: Put a piece of white construction paper on the newspaper work surface. Place twigs, leaves, berries, etc., in a pleasing arrangement on the paper. Spray the entire piece of construction paper and the items. If you like, lightly spray blue paint over the green to add the interest of a second color. Remove and discard the items.

Leader's Tip

Look in your children's library for *The Giving Tree,* by Shel Silverstein, a modern parable about self-sacrifice and happiness.

Growing Together

Small Group Activity: Exploring Sand

Invite participants to explore sand with one or more of these activities.

Sand Casting

Materials

> sand
> water
> molds: empty milk cartons, cottage
>   cheese containers, etc.
> pattern makers: twigs, shells, stones,
>   etc.
> either plaster of Paris or wax
> *Optional:*
> candle wicks

Invite participants to make sculptures or candles cast in sand. ***Directions to the participants:*** Mix sand with water until moist enough to hold together. Put the sand into a mold, such as an empty milk carton.

Use your hand to scoop out the design you desire, such as a hollow, in the sand. This design will be filled with plaster of Paris or wax. You can make a pattern on your design with twigs, stones, or other materials.

Either mix the plaster of Paris with water or melt the wax over hot water. Help the participants fill their designs with the plaster of Paris or the melted wax. (Wax molds can be made into candles with the addition of wicks.)

When the sculptures have hardened, have the participants lift the sculptures from the sand molds and brush off the excess sand.

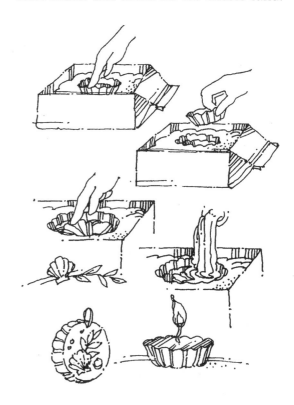

Sand Painting

Materials

> sand
> tempera paints
> paper towels
> paper cups
> heavy cardboard
> pencils
> glue
> plastic spoons
> paintbrushes
> spray can of shellac

Invite the participants to "paint" with sand. Have the participants mix sand with small amounts of tempera paint, spreading the sand onto paper towels to dry. Put the dried, colored sand into paper cups, using one cup for each color.

Give each participant a piece of heavy cardboard. *Directions to the participants:* Sketch your picture in pencil on the cardboard. Use a paintbrush to spread a small amount of glue on one area of the picture.

Use a plastic spoon to sprinkle the desired color of sand on the area with glue. Let the glue set for a few minutes; then turn the picture upside down. Tap the picture gently to remove excess sand.

Continue brushing glue, sprinkling sand, and removing the excess sand until your picture is finished. Let the picture dry completely before spraying it with shellac.

Sand Prints

Materials

> natural materials for printing: ferns, leaves, flowers, etc.
> paintbrushes
> glue
> construction paper in assorted colors
> sand

Invite participants to make Sand Prints of unusual shapes found outdoors. Ask the participants to find items that they wish to turn into prints: ferns, leaves, flowers, etc.

Have the participants brush glue onto one side of the desired items. Have each participant turn an item, glue side down, onto a piece of colored construction paper.

Have each participant press gently on the item; then carefully peel it off the paper. Have each participant sprinkle sand on the construction paper. Have the participants let the glue set the sand for several minutes before turning the papers upside down and gently tapping the papers to remove excess sand.

Growing Together

Small Group Activity: Exploring Weeds and Wildflowers

Invite participants to explore weeds and wildflowers with one or more of the following activities.

Bundled Grass Figures

Materials

sticks
string
scissors
grasses

Invite participants to make Bundled Grass Figures, which can be used as dolls or as characters in impromptu skits.

Directions to the participants: Use sticks and string to form a skeleton for your figure. Lay bundles of grass around the sticks of your figure. Tie the bundles to the sticks with string.

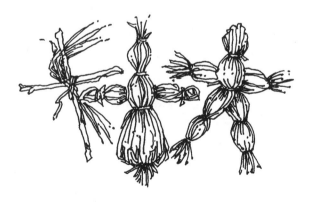

Plant Pictures

Materials

construction paper in assorted colors
scissors
glue
weeds, flowers, twigs, leaves, etc.
Optional:
felt pens

Invite participants to invent new plants from the plants available. This activity is suitable for either individuals or small groups.

Directions to the participants: Take a sheet of construction paper, scissors, and glue. Invent a new plant to place on your construction paper. Gather together grasses, weeds, flowers, twigs, etc. Use whatever parts you want from these plants to make a plant no one has ever seen before.

Glue your new plant on the construction paper. If you want, you may write a name for your new plant on the construction paper.

Creation Murals

Materials

weeds and wildflowers
large sheets of newsprint or butcher
  paper
decorative items: sand, rice, etc.
colored chalk
a variety of papers: metallic paper,
  colored tissue paper, rice paper,
  construction paper
rubber cement
scissors

Divide participants into three groups. Assign Psalm 148:1-6 to one group, Psalm 148:7-10 to the second group and Psalm 148:11-14 to the third group. Ask each group to illustrate its psalm verses by making a mural using any or all of the materials you have provided. Calligraphers might enjoy working words from the psalm into the design of the mural.

Closing Prayer

● Stand in a circle and sing the Doxology. Invite participants to close with a simple litany of thanksgiving. Ask them each to think of one blessing of creation for which they wish to give thanks. Go around the circle, allowing participants to name their chosen blessings of creation. Invite the rest of the participants to respond with: For *(chosen blessing of creation)* we praise you, Lord.

● Sing "All Creatures of Our God and King."

● Gather around the Creation Murals you made and read together Psalm 148. You may choose to read it:

— in unison.

— responsively, by dividing into two groups and alternating strophes.

— in choral fashion: by going around the circle, each participant reading a line

— each group reading the section that describes its mural and the whole group reading together the first and last line: Praise the Lord!

Assumption

Introduction and Information

The Blessed Virgin Mary is unique among the blessed. In one sense, she is the last of the Old Testament saints, one of God's faithful remnant who waits for the promised Messiah. In another sense, she is the first of the faithful, the Mother of our Lord and the Mother of the Church: the one whose "yes" to God invites into our world the Messiah who makes all things new.

Our last glimpse of Mary in scripture is found in Acts. She is in the upper room where, with the other disciples of her Son, she waits for the Comforter, who comes to dwell with her Son's Church forever.

Our knowledge of Mary is based on the biblical stories in which she figures, particularly the nativity cycle of stories found in the Gospel of Luke. These stories reveal a woman of courage and deep faith.

Mary's courage is revealed when she says yes to the bewildering invitation of God to bear the Messiah of her people and when she stands by the cross of her dying Son. Only faith in God could make such courage possible. As Mary lives with her holy child, she witnesses much that is mysterious, much that is as fraught with sorrow as with joy.

She hears the prophecy of Simon that sorrow will pierce her own heart, and the words of her 12-year-old Son that he must do his Father's work. Who knows how deeply Mary could grasp the nature of that work? All we do know is that Mary, the woman of faith, "treasured all these things in her heart" (Luke 2:51).

The Nativity Cycle

The stories of the Blessed Virgin Mary in the nativity cycle form a major part of the liturgy of the Church, beginning with the Feast of the Annunciation (March 25) and ending, not with Christmas, but with the Feast of the Presentation (February 2) when the infant Jesus is presented in the temple.

The Feast of the Annunciation on March 25 celebrates Mary's yes to God's invitation to bear the Messiah. At one time, the Church celebrated this date as the Christian New Year, since Mary's yes changed the course of human history and invited the eternal God to enter into human time.

The Feast of the Visitation, on May 31, celebrates Mary's visit to her pregnant cousin Elizabeth, a visit marked by songs and prophecies from the women. Even John the Baptist, yet to be born, leaped for joy in his mother's womb.

Growing Together

On January 1, eight days after Christmas, we observe the solemnity of Mary, the Mother of God. The liturgy for the day commemorates both Mary's part in the great gift of God's Son to God's people and the Name of Jesus, given eight days after his birth, according to Jewish law.

The Christmas season once lasted for 40 days of the Christian year, ending on the Feast of the Presentation on February 2. On this feast, Mary and Joseph bring Jesus to the temple in Jerusalem in fulfillment of the law. Here Mary and Joseph hear prophecies that again name Jesus the Chosen One of God.

This is a list of the Marian feasts of the calendar:
1. January 1—Mary Mother of God
2. February 11—Our Lady of Lourdes
3. February 2—Presentation of Our Lord
4. March 25—Annunciation
5. May—The Month of Mary
6. May 31—The Visitation of the Virgin Mary to Elizabeth
7. July 1—Immaculate Heart of Mary
8. August 15—The Assumption of the Virgin Mary
9. September 8—The birth of the Virgin Mary
10. September 15—Our Lady of Sorrows
11. October 7—Our Lady of the Rosary
12. November 21—The Presentation of Our Lady
13. December 8—Immaculate Conception of the Virgin Mary
14. December 12—Our Lady of Guadalupe
15. December 25—Christmas
16. December 31—The Holy Family

Marian Traditions

The activities and stories in this chapter could be used to celebrate any of the feasts named above, and some of the activities given are specifically aimed at some of these other celebrations. (The rosary activities would be especially appropriate in October celebrations of the rosary.) However, we especially commend to parishes a summer gathering held to honor Mary's Assumption, celebrated on August 15. We believe most parishes could welcome a chance for families to gather with one another in summer, before the hectic pace of the school year resumes.

On this day, some countries hold pilgrimages of light and song; other countries gather flowers in profusion. One medieval legend held that flowers regained the fragrance they had lost at the fall when Mary said yes to the conception of Jesus.

The proximity of August 15 to the harvest in many countries is marked by blessings of grain and other fruits of the earth. These seem especially appropriate when we think of the fruitfulness of Mary herself—not simply the physical fruitfulness of her fertility, but the spiritual fruitfulness of her courage and faith that bore fruit in the new covenant of Jesus. As we celebrate her feasts, let us thank God for her courage in saying yes to God and her faithfulness in bearing the fruit of that choice. Then let us listen to the words of Mary's Son as he says, "You did not choose me; I chose you and appointed you to go and bear much fruit" (John. 15:16).

Help! How do I plan this session?

How will I publicize this session?

_____

_____

How many people do I think might participate? _____

What are the ages of the participants?

_____

Where will we hold the session?

_____

Which recommended activities would work best with this particular group of participants? (Remember, we provide more activities than most groups can use in a single session. Pick a few that will work for your group.)

_____

_____

_____

_____

_____

_____

_____

_____

Volunteers

to do	names	phone numbers
planning:		
preparation and set-up:		
activity leaders:		
clean-up:		

Growing Together

Session

Gathering Prayer

Sing a Marian hymn or say together the Hail Mary.

Key Idea

Many biblical stories featuring the Blessed Virgin Mary are found in the nativity cycle of stories found in the Gospel of Luke.

Small Group Activity: Bible Study (for adult participants)

Materials

Bibles

Invite participants to study the lectionary readings for the Assumption of the Blessed Virgin Mary, August 15:

> 1 Corinthians 15:20-26
> Revelation 11:19, 12:1-6, 10
> Luke 1:39-56

Distribute Bibles to the participants and ask them to turn to Revelation 11:19, 12:1-6, 10. Invite one participant to read the passage aloud. Discuss:

- How do these verses describe God's people?
  - How do they describe the story of God's people as told in the Old Testament?
  - How do they describe the story of God's people as told in the New Testament?
- How do these verses describe the story of Mary?
  - How does the story of Mary reflect the story of God's people?
- How do these verses describe our own story?
  - How does our own story reflect the story of God's people?

Invite participants to work in small groups to discuss three more questions:

- Consider the story of God's people as a "sign in heaven." What signs of struggle can we find in the world today?
  - What signs of victory can we find in the world today?
  - What actions can we take as individuals or as a parish to support these signs of victory in the world today?

Ask the participants to turn to 1 Corinthians 15:20-26. Invite one participant to read the passage aloud. Discuss:

- What hope for God's people do we find in this passage?
  - How was this hope experienced in the life, death and resurrection of Jesus Christ?
  - How was this hope experienced in the life of Mary?

— How was this hope experienced in the life of other saints and heroes of faith?

— How do we experience this hope in our lives today?

● The writer uses the language of struggle and battle in this passage. What might have made such language useful to the early Church?

— What might make such language useful to the Church today?

— What concerns might such language cause to the Church today?

— How can we today honor these concerns as we study this passage?

Ask the participants to turn to Luke 1:39-56. Invite one of the participants to read the passage aloud. Discuss:

● What phrases in Mary's song describe her own victories?

— How did Mary experience God's power to bless?

— How did Mary experience God's power to do great things?

— How did Mary experience God's power to show mercy?

— How did Mary experience God's power to "exalt those of low degree"?

— How did Mary experience God's power to feed the hungry?

— How did Mary experience God's power to help God's people?

● What phrases in Mary's song describe the victories of God's people? *(Encourage participants to consider God's people in the Old Testament, the New Testament and the Church through the ages.)*

— How have God's people experienced God's power to bless?

— How have God's people experienced God's power to do great things?

— How have God's people experienced God's power to show mercy?

— How have God's people experienced God's power to "exalt those of low degree"?

— How have God's people experienced God's power to feed the hungry?

— How have God's people experienced God's power to help?

● What phrases in Mary's song describe our own victories?

— How have we experienced God's power to bless?

— How have we experienced God's power to do great things?

— How have we experienced God's power to show mercy?

— How have we experienced God's power to "exalt those of low degree"?

— How have we experienced God's power to feed the hungry?

— How have we experienced God's power to help?

Invite each participant to select one or more phrases from Luke 1:46-55 as their personal prayer statements. Encourage participants to paraphrase these phrases to apply more directly to their personal lives.

Growing Together

Leader's Resources: Outreach

- Ask families to collect and donate toiletries and personal items to a pre-natal clinic or a battered women's shelter. These items could be nicely wrapped and could include cards or letters affirming God's love for women.

- View the 15 minute video "We Learn from Mary: The Cloak of Many Colors" from St. Anthony Messenger Press and Franciscan Communications. Mary is depicted as a girl, woman, daughter, mother, disciple and companion who hears and brings God's word to others. Invite participants to explore how they can follow Mary as they consider the needs of the poor, the homeless and those in live in places in our world where there is armed conflict.

▶ Large Group Activity: Skits

Materials

Bibles

Invite participants to perform improvisational skits based on seven stories of Mary found in scripture. Divide the participants into seven groups. Assign each group one story:

- *Group #1:* The Annunciation
  Luke 1:26-38
- *Group #2:* The Visitation
  Luke 1:39-56
- *Group #3:* The Nativity
  Luke 2:1-7
- *Group #4:* The Shepherds' Visit
  Luke 2:8-20
- *Group #5:* The Presentation
  Luke 2:22-39
- *Group #6:* The Boy Jesus in the Temple
  Luke 2:41-52
- *Group #7:* The Wedding in Cana
  John 2:1-12

Directions to the groups: Have one member of your group read your assigned story aloud. Then ask all the members of your group to work together to devise a five-minute skit that tells your passage's story.

Allow 10-15 minutes for preparation. Then have each group present its skit to the other groups.

Key Idea

Traditional customs associated with the Blessed Virgin Mary include the rosary, and blessings of the harvest: fruits, flowers, and seeds.

Small Group Activity: Picture Rosary

Materials

> 8" x 11" drawing paper
> 5 sheets of 18" x 24" drawing paper
> felt pens or crayons
> tape

The rosary is a devotional method that employs meditation on certain scriptural stories—referred to as "mysteries"—combined with the recitation of certain set prayers, chiefly the Hail Mary, the Lord's Prayer and the Gloria.

Fifteen mysteries associated with Mary form the basis for the meditation. Five mysteries are devoted to the contemplation of joys Mary experienced; five mysteries are devoted to her sorrows; and five are devoted to glories she experienced. A set of beads is used in saying the rosary, providing a tangible aid to prayer.

Invite the participants to make a simple Picture Rosary reflecting the first five mysteries, those of joy: the annunciation, the visitation, the nativity, the presentation, and the finding of the boy Jesus.

Begin by dividing the participants into five groups. Give each group a Bible and ask one participant in each group to read aloud the story assigned to his or her group.

> *Group #1:* The Annunciation
>   Luke 1:26-38
> *Group #2:* The Visitation
>   Luke 1:39-56
> *Group #3:* The Nativity
>   Luke 2:4-20
> *Group #4:* The Presentation
>   Luke 2:22-39
> *Group #5:* The Finding of the Lost Child
>   Jesus in the Temple
>   Luke 2:41-52

Then ask the participants in each group to work together to make a picture of the story that they read. Distribute felt pens or crayons and a sheet of 18" x 24" paper to each group. Invite group members to co-operate in the design and completion of the picture. Allow 15-25 minutes for work.

When the participants are finished, arrange the pictures in a circle on a wall, placing them at an equal distance from each other. If possible, use the pictures to lead participants in praying together the rosary.

Growing Together

Small Group Activity: Flower, Fruit, and Seed Bouquets

Invite participants to make bouquets from the flowers, fruits, and seeds traditionally associated with the Assumption. Bouquets could be arranged beneath around pictures, statues or icons of Mary, or delivered to parish shut-ins to spread the joy of the parish celebration.

Note: In the Middle Ages, many flowers were considered symbolic of or sacred to the Blessed Virgin Mary. Barbara Damrosch, in *Theme Gardens*, lists pinks, carnations, sweet williams, iris, lavender, lilies, marigolds, pansies, roses, and violets as flowers appropriate to Mary.

Before the session invite participants who garden to bring flowers to the session. If no flowers are available from participants, carnations are the least expensive and most readily available fresh flower to use.

The bouquets below can correspond to specific feasts: Potpourri Baskets for winter or early spring feasts, such as the Annunciation; Tussie Mussies for late spring or early summer feasts, such as the Visitation; and Vases of Grass for late summer feasts, such as the Feast of Saint Mary on August 15.

Potpourri Baskets

Materials

> plastic mesh strawberry baskets
> ribbons in shades of pink, mauve, violet, etc.
> small oranges or tangerines
> cloves
> thimbles
> dried rose petals
> dried lavender petals

Note: Dried rose and lavender petals may be most inexpensively obtained in bulk, usually at natural food stores or herb stores.

These baskets may be made by individuals or small groups. *Directions to the participants:* Take a plastic mesh basket and weave ribbons in and out of the holes in the basket until the basket is covered with a pleasing design of ribbons.

Make a pomander by studding an orange or tangerine with cloves. Use a thimble to press the cloves deeply into the fruit. Set the pomander in the middle of the basket. Use the rose and lavender petals to make a nest for the pomander, alternating handfuls of petals in a pleasing design. For example, you might surround the pomander with a circle of lavender petals, then fill in the remaining spaces of the basket with rose petals.

Leader's Resources: Multicultural Issues

● In traditional Catholic devotions to Mary, she has often been referred to as "Our Lady." Gather together as many pictures of Mary as possible, using the best art available. Ask participants to consider some of the ethnic images of Mary: Our Lady of Guadalupe (Mexico), Our Lady of Lourdes (France), Our Lady of Fatima (Portugal), Our Lady of Czestochowa (Poland). Also ask participants to consider other traditional images of Mary: Our Lady of Grace, Our Lady of Perpetual Help, Our Lady of Sorrows, Our Lady of Peace, etc.

Discuss:
● What is the universal appeal of these images?
● How might we also be images of Mary in our daily lives? In our families?
● Which image of Mary do you find especially appealing? Why?

Tussie Mussies

Materials

small fresh flowers: pansies, violets, pinks, etc.
4" paper doilies
1/4" ribbons in assorted colors

Tussie Mussie is a name for an old-fashioned tiny bouquet, made with small, preferably fragrant, flowers, and decorated with ribbons.

Directions to the participants: Select several small flowers. Insert the flowers' stems through the center of a paper doily so that the flowers are arranged in a pleasing design. Use ribbons to decorate the Tussie Mussie with bows and streamers.

Growing Together

Vases of Grass

Materials

> wild grasses
> vases in assorted colors and shapes

Even wild grass can form a beautiful bouquet. Plants with seeds (representing fertility) were used in traditional customs for the Assumption. Grass that has formed seed heads provides an inexpensive source of these materials.

Invite the participants to begin with a gathering walk. Ask the participants to look for grasses that have formed seed heads. Ask the participants to look for both green and dry grasses.

When the participants return, provide them with a variety of vases. Invite each participant, or small group of participants, to choose one vase and to make a pleasing arrangement of grasses that matches the chosen vase. For example, a fat white vase may need a lush and thick bouquet of grasses, while a slender brown vase may look perfect with just a single stalk of dried grass.

Key Idea

The Feast of the Annunciation, on March 25, celebrates Mary's yes to God's invitation to bear the Messiah. Often coinciding with the last days of Lent, the feast has a feel of "Christmas in Lent." These activities are appropriate either for a celebration of the Annunciation or for extending the celebration of the Assumption.

Large Group Activity: Story

Tell this story of the Annunciation to the participants.

Mary Was Quiet

Mary, the maid of Galilee,
Mary lived by an ancient sea.
She had her dreams, her loves—her life;
she promised Joseph she would be his
   wife.

Mary grew quiet; Mary grew dark.
She held God's Word as God's own Ark.
Mary worked as women did.
She went to the market to shop and bid.
She sat with a spindle and spun sheep's
   wool.

She baked flat breads and set them to
   cool.
Mary was quiet; Mary was strong.
She could walk over hills all day long.
As Mary sat and worked one day
she heard God's herald Gabriel say,
"Mary, you are the chosen one
to bear God's Word, to birth God's Son."

Mary was quiet; we cannot know—
Was she afraid? Did she let it show?
"Let what God wants be done to me,"
said Mary, the maid of Galilee.

The angel left. She sat alone.
Did she touch her belly to feel her Son?
Mary was quiet; Mary was strong.
She knew God's Word could heal all
   wrong.

But did she think God's Word could die?
Did she know his cross? Did she start to
   cry?
Did she wonder why God would let it be
   so?
Mary was quiet; we cannot know.

Large Group Activity: Hymn Sing

Before the session arrange with one or
more musicians to lead the participants in
a hymn sing. Suitable music includes traditional songs in praise of the Blessed Virgin
Mary and Christmas carols that focus on
her part in the nativity stories. *Suggestions:*

   "Nova, Nova"

   "The Angel Gabriel from Heaven Came"

Large Group Activity: Good News Cards

Materials

   Bibles
   old Christmas cards
   scissors
   construction paper in assorted colors
   glue
   felt pens or crayons
   Optional:
   rice paper
   colored tissue paper
   metallic paper

Invite participants to make Good News
Cards to send to others on the Feast of the
Annunciation.

Begin by reading the story of the Annunciation to the participants, using the story
provided in this chapter or the biblical
story in Luke 1:26-38.

Distribute old Christmas cards, scissors,
and glue to the participants. Have the participants look for pictures suitable for illustrating the story of the Annunciation.

Ask each participant to make a new card
using cut-out pictures from the old cards
combined with drawings made with felt
pens or crayons. Participants may choose
instead to decorate their cards with one or
more symbols of Mary, as shown below.

Invite each participant to write a message
on the inside of the card that spreads the
good news told to Mary. Send the cards
home with participants for them to mail to
friends.

Growing Together

Small Group Activity: Angel Cookies

Materials

3/4 cup sugar

1/2 cup butter

1 egg

3/4 teaspoon vanilla

1-1/2 cups flour

1/8 teaspoon salt

1/2 teaspoon baking powder

icing (2 cups confectioners' sugar, 2-3 tablespoons milk, 1 teaspoon vanilla decorations: chocolate sprinkles, colored sugars, etc.)

Tools:

measuring cups and spoons

bowl

wooden spoon

flour sifter

rolling pin

cookie sheet

rack

plastic knives and spoons

Invite the participants to make Angel Cookies to celebrate the Feast of the Annunciation. This recipe makes three to four dozen cookies.

Directions to the participants: Put the butter and sugar into a bowl. Use the wooden spoon to cream the butter and sugar together. Beat in the egg and vanilla.

Sift together the flour, baking powder, and salt. Stir the flour ingredients into the butter mixture. (**Note**: The dough will roll out more easily if you allow it to rest in the refrigerator until chilled.)

Roll out the dough on a lightly floured surface. Cut out 2-inch angels with a cookie cutter or with a plastic knife. Put the cookies on a cookie sheet and bake at 325 degrees for about 10 minutes.

Put the cookies on a rack to cool. Mix together the confectioners' sugar, the vanilla, and the milk to make icing. When the cookies are cool, decorate them with icing, sprinkles, colored sugars, etc.

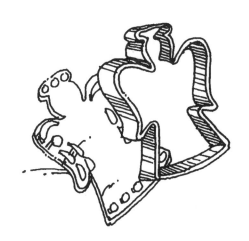

Key Idea

The Feast of the Visitation, on May 31, celebrates Mary's visit to her pregnant cousin Elizabeth, a visit marked by songs and prophecies from the women and a leap of joy from John the Baptist, yet to be born.

Small Group Activity: Story Writing

Materials

paper
pens or pencils

Tell the participants the following story of the Visitation (Luke 1:39-56). Then invite them to add to the story.

The angel Gabriel came to a young woman named Mary. The angel said, "Mary, you will bear God's Son to save all of God's people."

Mary said, "How can such a thing be? How can I bear God's Son?"

The angel said, "God's own Power will make it so. And here is a sign: Your cousin Elizabeth, even though she is an old woman now, is pregnant. God has made this possible."

Mary said, "I am God's servant. Let what God wants be done." And when the angel left her, Mary hurried over the hills to see her cousin Elizabeth.

Elizabeth saw Mary coming and went to meet her. Elizabeth called out, "The mother of my Lord comes to see me! Blessed are you, Mary, for believing God's promise. The baby in my womb is jumping for joy!"

Mary was glad to hear her cousin's words. Mary sang out, "I am filled with joy in the Lord because God has done great things for me." Mary stayed three months with her cousin Elizabeth and then returned to her own home.

After the Story

Invite the participants to compose stories that describe a day that Mary and Elizabeth spent together. They may enjoy setting their stories in the present day. Divide the participants into mixed-age groups of four or five participants. Give each group paper and pens or pencils, and ask one participant in each group to serve as the recorder.

Allow 10-15 minutes for work, then reconvene the group. Invite each small group to read its story aloud.

Growing Together

Large Group Activity: Visitation Poetry Festival

Materials

paper
pens or pencils

Before the session ask participants to bring favorite poems to read aloud. Parents of the youngest participants might be asked to bring their children's favorite nursery rhymes, too.

At the session explain that Mary sang a famous poem when her cousin Elizabeth hailed her and her holy child. Because of this, Thomas Merton called the Visitation the festival of all true poetry. Invite participants to celebrate Mary's poem by sharing their own favorite poems.

Begin the festival by reading Mary's song, the Magnificat (Luke 1:46-55). Then invite participants to follow with a reading of the poems they have brought.

Some participants might like to write their own poems in the session. Suggest some of the following forms:

Two-Word Poems: Though this poem may have as many lines as desired, each line should only have two words.

Examples:
Mother Mary
Jesus' mother
Holy virgin
Gentle woman
Obedient servant

Mary Acrostics: Write the name *MARY* vertically down the left side of a piece of paper. Make each line of the poem begin with a letter of her name and have it describe her in some way.

Example:
Mother of Jesus
Always obedient
Ready to serve
Your mother, too!

Haiku: This is a Japanese form of poetry that has three lines. It requires no rhyming, but is characterized by a specific syllable count for each line. The first and last lines should have five syllables; the middle line should have seven.

Example:
Mary is God's choice
To bear the Anointed One
And to do God's will.

Couplets: Some prefer the lyrical aspect of simple rhymes. Suggest that the participants try a few simple couplets, two lines that rhyme.

Examples:
Mary first prayed
Then she obeyed.
The angel was bright
And surrounded with light.
End the festival with this prayer:

Almighty God, whom the Blessed Virgin Mary praised in poetry, accept our poems today as praise of you, the Source of all poetry and praise; through Jesus Christ our Lord. *Amen*.

Small Group Activity: Bible Study (for older participants)

Materials

Bibles

Invite the participants to study the Magnificat by comparing it to the Song of Hannah. Distribute Bibles and ask the participants to turn to the Magnificat (Luke 1:46-55). Ask one participant to read the passage aloud or ask all the participants to read the passage aloud, either in a chorus or alternating between two groups.

Ask the participants to turn to the Song of Hannah (1 Samuel 2:1-10). Ask one participant to read the passage aloud or ask all the participants to read the passage aloud, either in a chorus or alternating between two groups.

Discuss:
- How are these two canticles similar? How do they differ?
- According to these canticles, what people does God favor?
  - What people today do you think God favors?
  - What evidence can you give from scripture to support your opinion?
  - What evidence can you give from your own experience to support your opinion?
- In what ways did Jesus fulfill the promises of these songs?

Divide the participants into small groups to discuss these questions:
- How do our own lives reflect the values of these songs?
- How does the life of our parish reflect the values of these songs?

Closing Prayer

- Distribute 3" x 5" index cards and invite participants to complete this sentence: *Holy Mary, Jesus' mother, is for me a model of...*

Close by reading the following prayer, pausing where indicated to allow participants the opportunity to thank God for Mary's example.

Lord, you are a great and good God. Your kindness to us is evident in all of life and most especially in your desire to redeem us through your Son, Jesus. Thank you for choosing Mary to hear your call and do your work. We thank you for the example she is to each of us. Like Mary, Lord, help us to be *(invite participants to read the words that they used to finish the sentence)*. *Amen.*
- Close by reading aloud the Magnificat responsively (Luke 1:46-55). Allow a few moments of silence for participants to add their own words of praise.

Bibliography

Achtemeier, Paul J., gen. ed. *Harper's Bible Dictionary*. San Francisco: Harper and Row, 1985.

Ball, Peter. *Adult Believing*. New York: Paulist Press, 1988.

Beasley, James R., Clyde E. Fant, E. Earl Joiner, Donald W. Musser, Mitchell G. Reddish. *An Introduction to the Bible*. Nashville: Abingdon Press, 1991.

Bergant, Dianne and Robert J. Karris, gen. eds. *The Collegeville Bible Commentary*. Collegeville, MN: The Liturgical Press, 1989.

Boadt, Lawrence. *Reading the Old Testament*. New York: Paulist Press, 1984.

Broderick, Robert C., ed. *The Catholic Encyclopedia*. rev. ed. Nashville: Thomas Nelson Publishers, 1987.

Brown, Raymond, et al. *The New Jerome Biblical Commentary*. Englewood Cliffs, NJ: Prentice-Hall, Inc. 1990.

Coffey, Kathy. *Experiencing God with your Children*. New York: Crossroad, 1997.

_____. *Hidden Women of the Gospels*. New York: Crossroad, 1996.

The Community of Women and Men in the Church: A Study Program. The Advisory Committee, Study on the Community of Women and Men in the Church. World Council of Churches. New York: Friendship Press, 1978.

Craghan, John F. *The Psalms: Prayers for the Ups, Downs, and In-Betweens of Life*. Wilmington, DE: Michael Glazier Books, 1985.

Cross, F.L. and E.A. Livingstone, eds. *Oxford Dictionary of the Christian Church*. 2nd ed. New York: Oxford University Press, 1974.

Dunning, James B. *Echoing God's Word*. Arlington, VA: The North American Forum on the Catechumenate, 1993.

_____. *New Wine, New Wineskins*. New York: Sadlier, 1981.

Ekstrom, Reynolds R. and Rosemary Ekstrom. *Concise Catholic Dictionary for Parents*. Mystic, CT: Twenty-Third Publications, 1982.

Fuller, Reginald H. *Preaching the New Lectionary: the Word of God for the Church Today*. Collegeville, MN: The Liturgical Press, 1984.

Gentz, William H., gen. ed. *The Dictionary of Bible and Religion*. Nashville: Abingdon Press, 1986.

Good News Bible: The Bible in Today's English Version. Catholic Study Edition. Nashville: Thomas Nelson Publishers, 1979.

Halpin, Marlene. *Imagine That! Using Fantasy in Spiritual Direction*. Dubuque: Wm. C. Brown Co., 1982.

Hamma, Robert M. *A Catechumen's Lectionary*. New York: Paulist Press, 1988.

Hiers, Richard H. *Reading the Bible Book by Book*. Philadelphia: Fortress Press, 1988.

Holmes, Urban T. *Ministry and Imagination*. New York: Seabury Press, 1976.

The Interpreter's Bible. George Arthur Buttrick, commentary ed. 12 vols. Nashville: Abingdon Press, 1955.

Irwin, Kevin. *Liturgy, Prayer and Spirituality*. New York: Paulist Press, 1984.

Kunkel, Fritz. *Creation Continues*. New York/Mahwah: Paulist Press, 1987.

Leech, Kenneth. *Soul Friends: The Practice of Christian Spirituality*. San Francisco: Harper & Row, 1977.

Lockyer, Herbert, Sr., gen. ed. *Nelson's Illustrated Bible Dictionary*. Nashville: Thomas Nelson Publishers, 1986.

McCauley, George. *The Unfinished Image. Reflections on the Sunday Readings*. New York: Sadlier, 1983.

McKenna, Gail Thomas. *Through the Year with the DRE: A Seasonal Guide for Christian Educators*. New York: Paulist Press, 1987.

McKenzie, John L., S.J. *Dictionary of the Bible*. New York: Macmillan, 1965.

Merton, Thomas. *Bread in the Wilderness*. Collegeville, MN: The Liturgical Press, 1953.

Metzger, Bruce M. and Roland E. Murphy. *The New Oxford Annotated Bible with the Apocryphal/Deuterocanonical Books*. New Revised Standard Version. New York: Oxford University Press, 1991.

Murphy, Irene T. *Early Learning: A Guide to Develop Catholic Preschool Programs*. Washington, DC: National Catholic Education Association. 1990.

Myers, Allen C., ed. *The Eerdmans Bible Dictionary*. Grand Rapids, MI: Wm. B. Eerdmans Publishing Company, 1987.

The New American Bible. Nashville: Thomas Nelson Publishers, Catholic Bible Press, 1987.

Peck, M. Scott. *The Different Drum: Community Making and Peace*. New York: Simon and Schuster, 1987.

Perkins, Pheme. *Reading the New Testament*. 2nd ed. New York: Paulist Press, 1988.

Peterson, Eugene H. *Answering God: The Psalms as Tools for Prayer*. San Francisco: Harper and Row, 1989.

_____. *Earth and Altar: The Community of Prayer in a Self-Bound Society*. Downers Grove, IL: InterVarsity Press, 1985.

Pfeifer, Carl J. and Janaan Manternach. *How to Be a Better Catechist*. Kansas City, MO: Sheed and Ward, 1989.

Rahner, Karl, ed. *Encyclopedia of Theology: The Concise Sacramentum Mundi*. New York: Crossroad, 1982.

Schippe, Cullen. *Planting, Watering, Growing!* Granada Hill, CA: Sandalprints, 1990.

Senior, Donald, gen. ed. *The Catholic Study Bible*. New York: Oxford University Press, 1990.

Shea, John. *Stories of Faith*. Chicago: Thomas More Press, 1980.

Sloyan, Gerard. *Commentary on the New Lectionary*. New York: Paulist Press, 1975.

Spivey, Robert B. and D. Moody Smith. *Anatomy of the New Testament*. 4th ed. New York: Macmillan Publishing Company, 1989.

Stott, John. *Basic Introduction to the New Testament*. Grand Rapids, MI: Wm. B. Eerdmans Publishing Company, 1964.

Stuhlmueller, Carroll, C.P. *New Paths through the Old Testament*. New York: Paulist Press, 1989.

_____. *The Psalms*. 2 vols. Old Testament Message Series, nos. 21, 22. Wilmington, DE: Michael Glazier Books, 1983.

Vanier, Jean. *Community and Growth*. 2nd rev. ed. New York: Paulist Press, 1989.

Walters, Thomas P., project director. *Director of Religious Education: Yesterday, Today and Tomorrow*. National Catholic Education Association. Silver Burdett and Ginn.

Ward, Carol. *The Christian Sourcebook*. rev. ed. New York: Ballantine Books, 1989.

Westerhoff, John H., III. *Will Our Children Have Faith?* NY: Seabury Press, 1976.

Wigoder, Geoffrey, gen. ed. *Illustrated Dictionary and Concordance of the Bible*. New York: Macmillan Publishing Company, 1986.

Resources for the Seasons and Feasts

Carey, Diane and Large, Judy. *Festivals, Family and Food*. Gloucestershire, England: Hawthorne Press, 1982.

Dunning, James B. *Echoing God's Word*. Arlington, VA: The North American Forum on the Catechumenate, 1993.

Halmo, Joan. *Celebrating the Church Year with Young Children*. Collegeville, MN: The Liturgical Press, 1988.

Luce, Clare Boothe, ed. *Saints for Now*. Harrison, NY: Ignatius Press, 1993.

Mathson, Patricia. *Pray and Play*. Notre Dame, IN: Ave Maria Press, 1989.

Nelson, Gertrude Mueller. *To Dance with God*. New York: Paulist Press, 1986.

_____. *To Celebrate: Reshaping Holidays and Rites of Passage*. Ellenwood, GA: Alternatives, 1987.

The Oxford Dictionary of the Christian Church. ed. F. L. Cross. Oxford University Press, 1958.

Pennington, M. Basil, O.C.S.O. *Through the Year with the Saints*. New York: Doubleday Publishing, Image Books, 1988.

Powers, Mala. *Follow the Year, A Family Celebration of Christian Holidays*. New York: Harper & Row Publishers, Inc., 1985.

Weiser, Francis X. *Handbook of Christian Feasts and Customs*. NY: Harcourt, Brace and World, 1958.

Resources for Prayer

deMello, Anthony. *Sadhana: A Way to God*. St. Louis: Institute of Jesuit Sources, 1978.

_____. *The Way to Love: The Last Meditations of Anthony deMello*. New York: Image Books, 1995.

Edwards, Tilden. *Living Simply Through the Day*. New York: Paulist Press, 1977.

Glover, Mary and Rob. *Our Common Life: Reflections on Being a Spouse*. Chicago: Acta, 1998.

Kastigar, Carole. *For Our Children's Children: Reflections on Being a Grandparent*. Chicago: Acta, 1998.

Meninger, William. *The Temple of the Lord: and Other Stories*. New York: Continuum Publishing Group, 1997.

Owens, Sherwood, III. *All Our Works Begun: Reflections on Being a Working Parent*. Chicago: 1998.

Pennington, M. Basil, O.C.S.O. *Awake in the Spirit*. New York: Crossroads, 1995.

_____. *Call to the Center: The Gospel's Invitation to Deeper Prayer*. New York: New City Press, 1995.

Strong, Dina. *Singular Ingenuity: Reflections on Being a Single Parent*. Chicago: Acta, 1998.

Taize Picture Bible. Philadelphia, Penn: Fortress, 1968

Learning Through Play

Fluegelman, Andrew, editor. *More New Games and Playful Ideas*. Garden City, NY: Doubleday, 1981.

_____. *The New Games Book*. New York: Pantheon, 1976.

Fry-Miller, Kathleen, Judith Myers-Walls, and Hanel Domer Shank. *Peace Works*. Elgin, IL: Brethren Press, 1989.

Gale, Elizabeth, editor. *Children Together*, Vol. 2. Valley Forge: Judson Press, 1982.

Glavich, Sr. Mary Kathleen, S.N.D. *Leading Students into Scripture*. Mystic, CT: Twenty Third Publications, 1987.

Griggs, Donald L. and Patricia Griggs. *Creative Activities in Church Education*. Nashville: Abingdon Press, 1984.

Griggs, Donald L. *20 New Ways of Teaching the Bible*. Nashville: Abingdon Press, 1977.

Halverson, Delia. *Teaching Prayer in the Classroom*. Nashville: Abingdon Press, 1989.

Hines, Rosemary Wesley. *The Idea Book*. Colorado Springs, CO: Meriwether Publishing, Ltd., 1981.

Orlick, Terry. *The Second Cooperative Sports and Games Book*. NY: Pantheon, 1982.

Peterson, Linda Woods. *The Electronic Lifeline: A Media Exploration for Youth*. Cincinnati: Friendship Press.

Priddy, Linda, Monte Corley, and Roy J. Nichols. *New Testament Bible Activities*. San Diego: Rainbow Publishers.

Rice, Wayne and Mike Yaconelli. *Play It!* Grand Rapids, MI: Zondervan Publishing House, 1986.

Schultz, Paul and Judith Wellington. *Caring for Creation*. Minneapolis: Augsburg Fortress, 1989.

Smith, Judy Gattis. *26 Ways to Use Drama in Teaching the Bible*. Nashville: Abingdon Press, 1988.

Wezeman, Vos. *Peacemaking Creatively through the Arts*. Brea, CA: Educational Ministries, Inc., 1990.

Ward, Elaine M. *All About Teaching Peace*. Brea, CA: Educational Ministries, 1989.

_____. *Be and Say a Fingerplay*. Brea, CA: Educational Ministries, 1982.